Many people have amazing stories to tell, but not everyone can wrap wonderful words around matters of the heart, drawing us in and letting us see, hear, taste, and feel the beauty rising from the ashes of her long-dead dreams. In *A Song in Every Silence*, Donna Paul lets readers ride along on her journey from a hidden sorrow to a joy she shouts from the rooftops, and she paints some breathtaking views along the way. Readers will come away with a sense that there's rhyme and reason to the seemingly tragic events of our lives.

—Jeanne Damoff,
author of *You and Me, Sister*
and *Parting the Waters*

With her captivating voice, Donna Paul leads you on an amazing journey to discover what it feels like to give your child away, then find unexpectedly he's been searching for you–for years, something your heart could have only imagined. A tender story of unwavering, sacrificial love. Well-told, humorous, and touching.

—Pamela Dowd,
author of *All Jingled Out*

A Song in Every Silence is a heart-wrenching story. Be prepared to experience a full range of emotions from tears and laughter to overwhelming compassion for the author and her son.

—Vickie Phelps,
author of *A Christmas Scrapbook*,
May Christ Be the Center of your Christmas,
Simple Pleasures,
101 Things to Be Thankful For

A SONG
IN EVERY
SILENCE

Donna G. Paul

A SONG IN EVERY SILENCE

The Story Behind "Hi Mom, it's Joel."

TATE PUBLISHING
AND ENTERPRISES, LLC

Published by Tate Publishing & Enterprises, LLC
127 E. Trade Center Terrace | Mustang, Oklahoma 73064 USA
1.888.361.9473 | www.tatepublishing.com

Tate Publishing is committed to excellence in the publishing industry. The company reflects the philosophy established by the founders, based on Psalm 68:11,
"The Lord gave the word and great was the company of those who published it."

Book design copyright © 2012 by Tate Publishing, LLC. All rights reserved.
Cover design by Joel Uber
Interior design by Nathan Harmony

Published in the United States of America

ISBN: 978-1-62147-085-4
1. Biography & Autobiography / Personal Memoirs
2. Family & Relationships / Adoption & Fostering
12.03.27

DEDICATION

To Wayne,
with love and gratitude for your unending support in
the telling of this story, for keeping my side of the bed
warm while I wrote, and all the while lending me your
steadiest hand in balancing my business and writing.

To Ron
for all the years of encouragement, memories, and education.

And to Joel, Jonathan, and Stephanie
for giving me such tender understanding and unconditional love.
It is my greatest honor to be your mother.

ACKNOWLEDGMENTS

For their unflagging support from the very beginning, my deepest thanks go to my family. Along the way, Dr. Stephen Yarbrough, Dr. Richard Hardoin, John Hoch and Cathy Walter, Phil and Margaret Ball, and the inimitable Kathy Patrick and her Pulpwood Queens of Jefferson, Texas encouraged my efforts. Special thanks to those writers who not only write with passion, but listened to my story at Girlfriend Weekends and encouraged me to keep writing: Mary McGarry Morris, Jeannette Walls, Michael Morris, Sam Bracken, Echo Garrett, Jim Ainsworth, Deeanne Gist, Nicole Seitz, and Texas 2010 Poet Laureate, Karla K. Morten. Thank you to my manuscript readers, Mary Dales, Patty Burger, and Connie Parker and my life-saving helpers, Kay McCann, Beverly Chisolm, and Paula Yates.

The Christian women of my critique group, Vickie Phelps, Pamela Dowd, Nanci Huyser, Jeanne Damoff, and Becca Anderson gently guided me into better writing. Nanci and I developed a special bond. She graciously took time out from her own writing to make excellent suggestions to my completed manuscript. Less than a week later, she was killed in an automobile accident. I will always miss her.

The North East Texas Writers Organization and East Texas Christian Writers' groups broadened my writing horizons by sharing their expertise, successes, and rejections.

My love and eternal gratitude go to Texas State Representative David Simpson and family, Dr. John Greene and his church family, Mims Chapel United Methodist Church, and my P.E.O. Sisters.

Love to editor Stacy Baker for welcoming me into the gracious Tate Publishing company with its unending support and joy at spreading words of God's grace. Conceptual editor James Bare is a kind and gifted soul who no doubt hides angel wings beneath his clothing.

Finally, there would be no story without Dr. and Mrs. Maurice Dewey, Joel's mom and dad, and his cousin Sarah. Most of all, I praise and love Shelley for standing strong in the shadows of Joel's twenty-year search for me.

FOREWORD

When Donna faced her crisis, I was a resident in ob/gyn at the University of Pittsburgh. Revolutionary changes in attitudes happening in the 1960s forced me to consider the significance of abortion. While in medical school from 1957 to 1961, the issue of abortion never came up. By the mid-1960s, it had become a hotly debated topic.

A terrible incident during my residency prompted me to take a stand and give serious consideration to the issue. One day while visiting operating rooms and observing various surgical procedures, I wandered into a surgical suite where a C-section had just been performed and a tiny two-pound infant delivered. Though making feeble efforts to cry and breathe, the baby was placed in a basin in a corner of the room. Everyone pretended they heard nothing—and soon the newborn grew silent. There and then, I knew there were profound and serious changes occurring in our society. Although abortions were illegal at the time, certain hospitals and physicians flaunted the law in order to promote legal changes.

Since abortion became legal with the *Roe v. Wade* decision in 1973, I have written extensively about the issue, both as a physician and member of congress. As a champion of liberty, I'm often challenged with the argument that a right-to-life position is inconsistent with protecting the private choices of pregnant women. This debate continues to rage even today, for it is a complex, emotional, and political issue. *However, if life itself cannot be protected, how can liberty and privacy be of greater importance?*

Some believe that if the Supreme Court had decided *Roe v. Wade* differently, or the current court would repeal the decision, the problems concerning abortion would go away. This simply is not so. *Roe v. Wade* only reflected the shifting moral attitudes of the 1960s. Our individual attitudes toward the sanctity of life must change if we hope to regain the proper respect that all life in every phase deserves.

Profoundly intimate and heart wrenching, this true story is fascinating. Donna faced a sad and lonely ordeal, but thirty-eight years of grim resolve led to a happy ending. Her story doesn't address any of the political and legal controversy surrounding abortion, which is why it sends a much more powerful message. She blames no one for her ordeal but embraces responsibility.

Reading *A Song in Every Silence* makes one keenly aware of the value and importance of a single life. I'm sure readers will find it difficult not to shed a tear or two, and it may be impossible *not* to come away with a greatly enhanced respect for life and personal responsibility.

—U.S. Congressman Ron Paul

I tell things as I remember them—not necessarily as they happened.

—Chuck Yeager

To those who remember events in a different way, I apologize in advance. It is not my intent to embellish, but to unfold a story that begs telling.

I endured decades of silent misery with a brave façade, trusting very few people with the knowledge that I ever looked back or suffered regrets. On the inside, I often doubted the biggest decision of my life. Like a child longing for the impossible, I wished things would change.

Forty years passed before I recognized that the special strength of hope from God's grace gave me courage. The courage to tell of what once remained unspoken, and how my suppressed sadness ended with one phone call—a call that changed dozens of lives forever.

PROLOGUE

September 15, 1965

By seven thirty Wednesday night, three regimented years of nursing school ended in a short walk across a stage. I received polite applause, a heavy-scented bouquet of pink roses, and a rolled-up diploma. My parents gave me a gleaming new dark teal Mustang.

Afterward, I clung to my father's strong shoulders, not wanting to let him go to his other family. I noticed brimming tears as he turned to his car. "Good night, Daddy. Thank you so much—for everything. I love you." Whispering into the dark, I waved until the taillights disappeared. "Good-bye, Dad… I'm sorry."

Saturday morning at Mom's, I forced a laugh while I hugged her good-bye, lingering a few minutes longer than usual. Before I lost the last of my resolve, I climbed into the driver's seat, cranked up the radio, gunned the Mustang, and roared down Fulton Street. I couldn't get away fast enough.

Making a turn west, I caught my reflection in the mirror: dark curly hair and fair skin. Audrey Hepburn sunglasses hid my tear-filled eyes. I pulled a stick of Dentyne from my madras clutch, thumbed it open, and popped the dusty red rectangle into my mouth. Sharp, biting cinnamon stung my nose, made me gasp in mild surprise. I felt better.

I was twenty-one, all grown up, and finally, finally, I was a nurse. I smiled at the headiness of graduation, a new car, moving, and becoming a nurse.

My car closed in on its shadow. I passed a rest area and glimpsed a little girl skipping beside a tall man. His hand held hers. I'd bet she felt loved and safe with her daddy. If everything had been okay, I would have considered myself like her—one lucky girl.

Lovin' Spoonful crooned, and I sang along, "Do you believe in magic?" Losing myself in it, I floated above the circumstances threatening my happiness. I trusted with all my heart the wonderful life I'd always dreamed of waited around the next bend.

I yawned as foliage along the roadside blurred into long ribbons of faded green. If it'd been a normal day, the monotonous thumping of the tires might make me pull over. I lifted my foot from the accelerator, reconsidered, shoved it down again.

This crisp fall day was far from ordinary. Everything was not okay.

When I turned up the radio, a familiar fluttering low in my belly jolted me back to my private world. I hadn't told a soul—none of my friends, no family members, not even my sweet mother. Even if he'd called, I wouldn't have told the young man who took away all my dreams. Since the date rape, my engagement ring no longer covered its indentation on my finger. Shame swelled inside me until tears left wet spots on my lavender sweater.

As BJ Thomas sang, a stronger flicking came from the baby inside me. My hand flew to cinch the lap belt tighter to keep him safe. I snuffled through BJ's lyrics, "Don't worry, baby." My heart knew I carried a boy. It also knew nothing could ever be all right again.

I am not fit to be a daughter, a wife, or a nurse.

Another tiny wriggle.

How can I possibly be your mother?

CHAPTER ONE

May 1949

Squinting from the sunshine, I held up the heavy towel from the basket between us. "Tell me that story again, Mommy."

"What story, Donna?"

"You know—the one where you and Daddy got married two times." The towel, flattened from the wringer atop the washer flopped over onto my extended arm.

Momma took two clothespins from the striped bag and held them in her teeth. She spun the squealing arms of the clothes rack to an empty row of plastic cords, gave the mint green towel a resounding snap, and pinned the corner to its yellow neighbor.

"After he finished teaching one afternoon, your father picked me and Aunt Blanche up at Grandma's. We were going to get married—in secret! We didn't have money for a fancy wedding, but the big reason we didn't tell anyone was that your Grandma Granger believed in church weddings."

I sat up straight and crossed my legs Indian style.

"We got married on Friday, January thirteenth, nineteen thirty-three, at city hall, in front of a justice of the peace. It wasn't a big ceremony with flowers and everything. We just promised we would love each other. Your aunt Blanche was so excited she kept giggling, which of course made me giggle."

Smiling, Momma looked down at me as she came close and picked out another towel. "You know, twins do things like that sometimes. If I fell down and skinned my knees, Blanche cried. If she got a tummy ache, my stomach hurt. If we were talking in bed when we were supposed to be asleep and Grandpa hollered up the stairs for us to be quiet, we both laughed until one of us got spanked."

She let out a snort. "Grandpa spanked whoever was on the side of the bed nearest the door. If Blanche got it, she'd cry and say, 'You sleep on this side tomorrow.'

"The next night we'd switch sides, get to giggling again, and Grandpa would charge up the stairs. He didn't turn on the light, so he didn't know which of us he'd get, but he'd race around to the far side of the bed, grab that girl, and give her a good spank. It was usually poor Blanche. I always let her choose which side she wanted..."

Mom's laughter bubbled up until it brought tears to her eyes.

Laughing along with her, I rolled over onto my tummy and brushed my palm over the thin blades of grass beside me.

"Anyway, when your aunt Blanche went home and shared the news of our secret wedding, everyone was delighted. My whole family loved your daddy. Your other grandparents liked me too, but Grandma Granger felt we weren't really married. She put her foot down, hard, like this." She stomped the grass flat next to me.

"Six months later, she and Grandpa led their friends on a nine-hour trek to New Jersey. Your daddy and I got married again—dressed in proper wedding clothes, in church, in front of seventy guests."

Begging Momma to tell me more, I sat up to choose a white towel with a tear at the edge and waved it in her general direction.

"When your daddy was in college, he worked every summer as a deck hand on a steamboat on Lake George. During school semesters, he earned money as an organist for a church miles away from school. He drove a Model T Ford with skinny little tires about this big." She made a gap between her thumb and first finger the width of half a clothespin.

She turned from the rack and smiled. "You know how we laugh when your brothers try to ride their bikes through ice patches on the sidewalk? Well, every Saturday afternoon, your daddy skidded and slid along those frozen roads for three hours to get to the church.

"When he arrived, he built a fire in the wood stove, warmed his hands, and then rehearsed the music for the next morning. When it got late, he dragged a pew up close to the stove to sleep on. He used his wool overcoat for a blanket."

Momma's back was to me again, but I saw her shoulders hunch forward in a little shudder. "He says it was ice cold in that church at night. No matter the weather though, he never missed a service." She got quiet for a minute then talked about how Dad graduated from Crane School of Music, became a high school music teacher in New Jersey, and met her at a faculty dance. After they married, he taught voice and piano lessons at home, took night classes at Columbia University, and earned a master's degree in music.

While I waited—I knew the best part came next—I picked at a scab on my knee and then stretched out on my back. I folded my hands beneath my head and watched the clouds scoot past a hundred miles above us.

"When your brother was still in my tummy at the hospital, your dad paced a while and then announced in a rather gleeful voice, 'Well, it's time for me to go home to teach a couple of lessons.' Back then, fathers didn't hang around the hospital except for maternity visiting hours. Knowing your father all too well, I gave him strict instructions as he headed toward the door."

Hair glinting golden red, she turned to me in the sunlight and wagged her finger, "'Now, Stanley, I don't want you to buy a piano, a dog, or a new car while I'm in the hospital.'"

Mom grunted as she bent over the laundry basket and tugged out the last twisted sheet. "Guess what happened?"

I giggled as I ticked off the answer. "You brought home Dale, and got a new car, a piano, and an Irish setter puppy."

Nodding and smiling down at me, she propped the basket on her hip as we walked back to the porch.

• • •

Grandma Granger kept the books for the burial vault business she and Grandpa owned. After he died of a heart attack at a cemetery, Grandma struggled to keep the business going with a few workers and a foreman.

As a teacher, Dad didn't have to go into the service during World War II, but he answered his call of duty to help his mother. Our family moved to upstate New York in 1944. We traveled in the car he'd bought when Momma had Dale. I was an infant, Dave was four, and Dale was eight. Our Irish setter sat in the back seat between my brothers. The piano came on a truck my uncle drove.

Whenever she told me about moving, Momma always said, "You were only four months old, Donna, so I held you in my arms the whole trip. It was a very long trip, but I was happy because I finally had a little girl."

I loved hearing the part about being a baby in my mother's arms.

Settling us in an old brick house in Glens Falls, Dad threw himself into expanding the business. While he worked six days a week, his music career dwindled to church organist and choir director. Mom decorated the house with antiques from Grange Hall rummage sales.

A little later, Dad indulged his desire for a place on the water and bought us a small summer camp on Copeland Pond. I don't remember the house, but I do recall standing, my navy blue wool bathing suit dripping onto the dock, as Mom checked me for leeches when I got out of the water.

The consummate daddy's girl, I couldn't wait for him to come home from work. In our evening routine, I'd rush to him for my bear hug, burying my face against his dark green work shirt. Like his trucks and skin, his clothes reeked of cherry pipe tobacco, tar, and cement dust. I never minded those scents; they were as much a part of Dad as his musical gifts, rough hands, and dimpled grin.

In the course of a workday, grease and tar toughened the skin of his hands. Dark residue permeated every line of his palms and fingers, packing each nail bed full. He scrubbed his hands with Lava soap before dinner.

After dinner, I'd pull off Dad's tan L.L. Bean work boots then hand him his sheepskin-lined slippers. He'd massage in great gobs of Pond's Cold Cream to loosen any lingering grime, slip onto the piano bench, and limber his stiffened fingers by playing popular tunes by ear. I grew up sitting next to him, belting out every verse of "Heart of My Heart," "Swing Low, Sweet Chariot," and his favorite, "Danny Boy."

While he played, Mom read in her wing-back chair beside the piano. During difficult preludes, Dad would utter a little curse under his breath and repeat the same few measures while admitting, "I can hear every note I need to play, but my fingers are so stiff they can't keep up." When he finished, he lit his pipe, grabbed the *Glens Falls Post Star* newspaper, and headed for his favorite red leather chair.

At age four, I knew without a doubt I'd be a nurse when I grew up. I made certain everyone who asked understood as well. Daddy was my favorite patient. Either he didn't really mind the bandages and ministrations, or he was too tired to object. I poked and prodded, made him tell me where he hurt, and gave him dozens of shots. I asked him to stick out his tongue and say, "Aaah." He'd open his mouth wide and sing a scale instead.

"Daadddy," I'd complain. "You have to just say what I tell you." He'd then deliver one very long "aah."

Evenings ended for me as my father tucked me into bed, whispering, "Good night, my little chickadee."

"I'm not your chickadee, Daddy. I'm your nurse, remember?"

He stood in the doorway while I turned to the wall with the nursery rhyme wallpaper and fell deep into the sleep of the innocent, filled with dreams of waking to a wonderful pony in our backyard.

• • •

My father played organ with his feet and left hand, directing each of his three Episcopal church choirs with the other. I sang in the children's choir at the early service, skipped across the street for Sunday school, and then reclaimed my spot on the organ bench for the late service.

After church Dad hung up his black organist's robe, straightened his tie, and shrugged into his suit coat. He buttoned the double-breasted jacket and winked at me as he put on his hat at a jaunty angle. I leaned against his big shoulder, humming my favorites: "The Little Brown Church in the Vale" and "Jesus Loves Me" as he drove us home to Sunday dinner. I hoped Dad noticed I had a clear voice and pronounced every word just right.

In the spring of 1949, Dad bought a much larger cottage. The day after school let out, we headed up Route 9 to the lake. Mom and us kids stayed at our Whispering Pines cottage until Labor Day. Dad came up on weekends. I lived in bathing suits, rarely exchanging them for shirts and shorts. The numbing waters of beautiful Lake George warmed to a cold seventy degrees by August, but I spent every moment I could in it—graduating from a doggy paddle to a choppy crawl stroke.

Late Friday afternoons, my young collie's pricked ears gave advance warnings of Dad's Dodge Power Wagon grinding its way down our road. Barking with excitement, Prince ran ahead as I charged up the steep stairs to the parking area where I leapt into my father's arms to receive his familiar-scented hug.

Once he'd greeted my mother with a kiss, I sat next to him, still in my bathing suit, blue-lipped and shivering, as we sang from a worn red velvet-covered organ bench. Our songs carried over Mom's pot-clanging, dish-thudding dinner preparations. Dad pumped the wheezing antique pump organ pedals up and down until our music filled the night.

Lake George summer residences passed down through generations of families. Few telephones existed in the cottages of the fifties, many still had outhouses, and everyone's cold drinking water came from the crystal-clear lake. Complete sets of summer friends bonded together by a carefree life on the lake. Neighbors came to call unannounced, on foot or by water.

I knew every neighboring family, the inside of all of their homes, and the creaks of their porch steps as well as I did my own. I knew every rut, rocky area, and protruding root of the trail between camps and never needed a flashlight to find my way home in the dark.

Each summer Mom's relatives came from New Jersey for vacation, and our porch filled with camaraderie and laughter. My father teased my cousins constantly. He'd hide someone's dessert or drink their lemonade while they looked for a mysterious mouse behind their chair. Still, they all loved "Uncle Stanley." Tiny Grandma Schoonover sat in the shade, swallowed up in a red Adirondack chair. She watched quietly as Mom taught my cousins and neighbor kids to swim. Pretending to practice my strokes, I showed off nearby.

One summer I spent hours watching my father and Dale build a large dock with a u-shaped slip for our two wooden motorboats. They covered the entire structure with a sundeck, added a canvas-covered diving board, and a guest changing room beneath the deck stairs. Later, on the slope outside Mom's kitchen window, they built me a red playhouse, complete with white-trimmed windows and a tiny porch.

A child's Blue Willow tea set and red tin dishes sat on a small table, ready for the next visitor. Momma was my most frequent guest. Sipping our pretend tea on the playhouse porch, we watched clouds high above the towering pines. She had exotic endings to "That cloud looks like a…" I saw horses, ponies, and puppies. Mom saw images of a woman with a parasol, a fluffy duckling, or the sails of a pirate ship.

My mother entertained steady streams of summer guests. She sewed curtains for the cottage, the changing room, and my playhouse. She made pom-pom fringed tablecloths with matching plaid napkins, and every August, while I fidgeted and fussed at the pins and fittings, she sewed fall school dresses for me.

• • •

I kept "lake books" on my bedside table for rainy days: *The Bird's Christmas Carol, Maida's Little House,* and *The Five Little Peppers and How They Grew.* Mom read them aloud, never admonishing me for coloring inside. As I learned to read, I carried the books to sit near her in the toasty-warm kitchen. Momma made us comforting roast chicken and biscuits, ham-filled pea soup, or Spanish rice with Johnny cake baked in a cast-iron skillet.

Sometimes after supper, Dad would load us in our long mahogany Hackercraft and back it out of the slip for a ride. Behind the gleaming bow, there was a leather seat for three in the front and a hatch, glossy with marine varnish, separated a similar seat aft. Mom sat in the front, I perched on Daddy's lap to help steer, and Dale and Dave rode in the back. Prince voiced his displeasure in loud woofs and raced beside us along the shore. Once out of the bay "the Hacker" flew over slapping waves as Dad pushed the flat throttle lever up, coaxing speed from its big engine. Standing with my head no longer protected behind the windshield, my hair stung my face as it whipped in the rushing air.

Coming home at night on the quiet lake, Dad eased down the throttle as we entered our bay. Winking house lights shone from among the trees. We glided through inky black water reflecting our red and green bow lights—our trailing wake a ghostly white, roiling streak. Lulled by the engine idling in a throaty, subdued roar, I slumped against Daddy and fought to stay awake.

Tired and happy, I dropped my still-damp bathing suit on the floor and went to bed to dream again of my pony-now-turned-horse.

By each Labor Day, Momma would pack my new school dresses, and I'd force my feet back into the dusty shoes that waited through the summers beneath my bed.

• • •

A stickler for manners like prim and proper Grandma Granger, my father made sure we behaved at meals. Without warning, he'd reach over to thump a funny bone with the handle of his knife if he caught one of us with an elbow on the table.

Some evenings the five of us piled into our 1950s Woody station wagon and went out to eat. His standards applied whether we had a three-course Italian meal on white linen tablecloths or giggled through root beer mustaches over hot dogs at Zack's, our favorite roadside stand.

Dad left home in June—a month before I turned twelve. He never said good-bye; he never explained. He left that to my mother.

Chapter Two

With Dad gone, our family disintegrated as summer approached. Momma, of course, was devastated. Dale left college to study voice in New York City. Dave turned into a bitter sixteen-year-old who sulked about and spent much of his time in the loft bedroom he'd fashioned above the garage. Once I realized that Daddy—the father I couldn't get enough of—wasn't coming home, I withered from a happy little girl into a miserable, bratty juvenile. Unable to understand he'd left my mother, I felt alone as I suffered his absence.

Dad sold our Whispering Pines cottage to buy the farm, a forty-acre property nine miles away. For the first time in my life, I wouldn't spend the summer at the lake, enjoying our usual friends, company, and fun. Worst of all in my preteen myopia, after waiting years for my turn, I wouldn't be learning to drive either of our classy inboards.

Our house in Glens Falls became "Mom's house." Over a hundred years old, it had no insulation in its lathe and plaster walls. Its brick exterior retained the sun's heat through the sultry nights. In my sweltering bedroom, I cried myself to sleep. I resented every moment with my mother. Mourning the loss of my daddy, carefree summers, and the security of two parents, I openly blamed her for everything I felt.

Youthful innocence shielded me from Dad's indiscretions, but Mom endured public humiliation, Dave's insolence, and my wrath. I never saw her cry. She never raised her voice to us. She may have wept in the privacy of her bedroom as we forged a new trail from the country club to the poor house, but she walked with grace in our community. She taught me a lasting lesson by never disparaging my father.

By early July, in part to alleviate my sigh-punctuated boredom, as well as to supplement her sporadic support checks, Mom arranged a full-time babysitting position for me. I learned to care for a neighbor's two-year-old son and be a responsible employee.

Dave didn't have to get a job. My mother either couldn't make him or worried about his continuing bad behavior enough not to ask him. He lived in a world of comic books above the garage where he read for hours and learned to smoke cigarettes. My brother loved the sound of changing letters around in words—cat and mouse would become "mat and couse"; bread and butter, he'd pronounce "bed and brudder." Thus, Dave Granger prophetically became Grave Danger.

Dave had always teased me, but now he turned more to physical restraint when Mom wasn't home. Several times a week he came after me. He seemed to boil over with frustration at the ugly changes in his life. He was tall and gangly, and my determined struggles availed little. He'd hold his palm against my forehead, keep his long arm straight and bend forward just enough so none of my punches reached his body.

When I no longer had the strength to swing, I hollered "Uncle" as he pinned me against the wall. He wouldn't free me until I sobbed in sheer desperation.

· · ·

My mother's divorce attorney helped her open a checking account and taught her how to write her first check. Grandma Granger had always paid our bills, and it took months for Mom to learn which ones to pay first, which to delay, and that she needed to keep funds for groceries. At age forty-five, with no business skills, Mom acquired her own job working as a seamstress in an exclusive dress shop. Clothing of the fifties included adequate seam allowances, but altering expensive suits was exacting and nerve-wracking. Workers paid for tailoring mistakes at full retail. Monday through Saturday she limped four blocks home from downtown in the high heels required for work. Exhausted, she'd kick off those shoes by the front door, peel off her gloves, drop them into her handbag, and collapse on the sofa.

Her one good pair of precious stockings dripped from the bathroom towel rack every night. She had a single nylon left as a spare—inside folded white tissue paper in its flat stocking box tucked in her top dresser drawer.

Not long after she began working, Mom sat me down for a talk about our life together. "I can't do everything, honey. From now on, you'll have to be a big girl and make our suppers when you get home from your job. I don't care what it is—as long as it's hot and on the table on time. You'll be in charge of the shopping and cooking supper. I'll do cleaning and laundry."

Dave remained responsible for the comic books and sneaking cigarettes.

Handling the food budget, such as it was, swelled my twelve-year-old head. I swaggered to our small neighborhood market the next Saturday and indulged my sweet tooth. Our charge account grew but not from entrée selections. We struggled through the week, eating the odd combinations of canned foods I concocted from the back of our kitchen cupboards. The second week didn't turn out much better because I'd made foolish choices again.

Privy to a steady stream of neighborhood talk, the grocers, Mr. and Mrs. Sweet, took pity on our family after watching me buy the second load of Pepsi and chocolate chip cookies we could ill afford. When I confessed I was now the cook as well as the family shopper, Mr. Sweet took special interest.

One Saturday morning in July, I closed the tinkling front shop door and crossed the few steps to where Mr. Sweet worked cutting meat on a four-legged chopping block. Blending with the scent of fresh beef, I smelled the sawdust covering the floor near the wide wooden door of the meat locker.

He put down his cleaver and greeted me with his cheerful "Guten Morgen, Donna." After wiping his hands on his apron, his bald pink head disappeared behind the meat case. Through the glass I watched his muscular arm reach inside to pull out a cut of beef.

"I saved this nice one just for you." As he wrapped the roast in white butcher's paper and tied it with string, he instructed me how to cut it into chunks then brown it with yellow onion slivers. The resulting meat would stretch into three meals—a stew, stroganoff, and vegetable beef soup.

Mrs. Sweet helped me find noodles, sour cream, and the fresh vegetables I'd need and recorded my purchases. She winked as she tucked two bananas and a long, waxy cucumber into the paper grocery bag. She didn't add them to my ticket.

Most evenings Mom seemed so tired she didn't pay attention to what I served, but after serving a new convenience, boxed macaroni and cheese, I took Mrs. Sweet's advice to heart. Not only was made-from-scratch food less expensive, but aged Vermont cheddar cheese added to white sauce made a much tastier macaroni dish. Through these kind people, when I paid our account on the first of each month, I came to a gradual understanding what "budget" meant.

Although Mom once drove, she hadn't had a license since leaving New Jersey. Of course, now we couldn't afford a vehicle. We also couldn't afford a dentist, the movies, or the newspaper.

• • •

That summer I also learned I'd see my father on a regular basis—at choir practice on Wednesday nights, as well as every weekend. I packed my small suitcase as soon as I finished babysitting each Friday. I also saw Prince, who now lived at The Farm with Dad.

Picking me up at Mom's one afternoon in mid-July, he took me to a neighboring community for a "birthday surprise." I suppose to soothe my wounded spirit, although neither of us had a single hour of experience with them, he bought me the horse I'd dreamed of all my life.

A sleek six-year-old bay mare, Sheba had a saddle-shaped area of white hair above her withers. Dad extolled the virtues of responsibility that came with pets. "I expect you to feed her every morning. It's up to you to make sure she stays healthy. She'll need grain and hay and lots of water. You'll have to brush her and comb her mane and tail, and…"

I half-listened, riding the nine miles back to the farm with my head twisted around, watching the borrowed trailer sway along behind us. I had great difficulty believing the trailer held the most beautiful horse I'd ever seen.

Sitting atop a large wooden gate, I forgot my past months' misery for the moment as I watched Sheba graze in her paddock. I was enthralled. Every ripple of my very own horse's skin, stomping of her foot, or flicking at flies with her long black tail fascinated me. I watched her until it became too dark to see.

I hardly slept that night. As soon as the sun rose above the tree line, I tore down the path to the lower barn level. Still there, Sheba continued to nibble the grass, stomp her feet, and flick her tail.

Dad returned the empty trailer and came back with sandwiches, two bottles of Coke, and the second half of my present—the first one hundred bales of hay. While we watched Sheba, we ate our lunch on a grass slope. Afterward, Dad had me pull each sixty-pound bale off the truck. I sang as I started dragging bales into an old pen on the main floor of the barn. By about bale number five I no longer sang, I just sweated. Already responsibility hit hard.

Dad also brought a sack of feed that he dumped into the grain storage box beside the stall. He handed me a small wooden bucket to use when I fed Sheba her oats. The yellow bucket seemed to be the only item he saved when he'd sold our fully furnished cottage, antique pump organ and all.

The Farm perched on the side of a mountain and overlooked about half of the twenty-six miles of Lake George. Despite a few mishaps, I became more at ease in the saddle and spent hours exploring the mountain's abandoned logging trails. By now, Prince no longer barked in alarm when I climbed into the saddle. Alert and regal, he trotted ahead, plumed tail arched over his back.

My favorite route led to an old reservoir. The deep pool, walled in lichen-covered rock, filled a wooded glade that remained quiet much of the time except for the occasional chirp of a flitting cardinal. Sheba grazed and drank cold water while I sat on the wall of the reservoir, enveloped in the solitude of the forest. There, I grew up enough to accept that my father hadn't left *me* after all.

While I rode on weekends, Dad spent afternoons renovating the old farmhouse. I heard the noises of his hammer and saw from miles away as he laid the subflooring in a new, forty-foot-long living room. As he had at the homes he shared with my mother, Dad built a fireplace—this one with a stone facing. Befitting the large living room, the firebox had a huge five-foot opening. I loved this big room and envisioned how a new piano would look in one corner, with a tall Christmas tree—decorated by the two of us—in the opposite one.

As was our habit, Dad and I sang together in the quiet evenings, but he seemed distracted and distant. I would catch him staring out his picture windows at Lake George far below. He didn't share why he left home—or that he'd soon remarry. He may not have thought of his twelve-year-old daughter as someone with whom he could share his thoughts or plans, but his silence taught me how to hurt those I would later love.

Chapter Three

No matter how daunting her life, Mom tried to sound cheerful. She smiled as she reassured my brother and me that she and Dad both loved us. Demonstrating how to look for the humor in life, she'd shake her head and say, "It's ironic your father and I married the first time on Friday the thirteenth—that's the date we divorced too."

In the kitchen, Momma lifted the lids from the pots on the stove to survey my latest concoction. The woman who had basked in the sun on the dock every summer I can remember had a pale face that July. As she stirred the mixed vegetables with a long wooden spoon, her eyes held a faraway look, as though remembering pots brimming with food for five. We filled our plates with supper. She took less food than Dave and me, saying, "I'm just not very hungry tonight." There were never leftovers to put away.

Dave withdrew more and more, but when he emerged from the garage, he often headed straight for me. Hearing him bang as he came in the back door, I made myself small and still. It didn't matter—he found me no matter where I was. He picked fights over the television show I watched, the chair I sat in, or my time in the bathroom.

Reliving her workday with a friend, Momma would call out from the den, "*Please* stop all that yelling." As soon as she started talking on the phone again, Dave resumed his efforts with quiet vigor.

Malicious gossip about my unfaithful father and "poor, poor Eleanor" spread from our neighborhood through the entire town like southern kudzu. My parents' divorce became my social homicide when I took a first nervous step across the junior high threshold. The friends I'd gone to parties with, taken dance class with, and invited to the lake didn't speak to me. I lost popularity—in fact, I ceased to exist in their eyes. I couldn't figure out what I'd done wrong. It seemed impossible my *mother* would understand, and lonesome cries from my secret heart remained mute.

To add to my humiliation I'd gained several inches, as well as a few pounds during the summer, outgrowing all my clothes except for one blue dress. My mother sewed all through my childhood—and now at work—but sadness, loneliness, exhaustion, and the brutal responsibilities thrust upon her rendered her incapable of opening her Singer cabinet.

Girls wore dresses to school then, and with no money for new ones, Mom brought home a friend's used dress and hemmed it. The dress was an orange and black print with a smocked bib and pleated skirt. I remember it well—as the second of two dresses I endured wearing that entire school year.

Junior high combined pupils from three elementary schools. The large number of students, differing routines, and changing classes catapulted me into a constant state of confusion. I didn't own a notebook to organize class locations and teachers' handouts, so I scrawled reminders to myself and slipped them into my textbooks.

For months, I either lost the most recent schedule I'd requested a day or two earlier at the office or, in a panic, couldn't remember exactly where my locker was. If I did find it, I couldn't recall my combination to retrieve the reminders inside books from an earlier class. Whenever I managed to open the lock, I'd stand in front of my locker in a stupor, gazing at the big books piled inside, trying to figure out which class could possibly be next.

I dreaded the sound of each bell—it signaled the terror of trying to find my way again. I couldn't seem to grasp what was supposed to be my own routine.

Unlike the majority of the girls in my gym class, my favorite activity was swimming. Dressed in ugly "old-timey" swimsuits, we swam two days a week. I seldom remembered which ones.

On the wrong day, or at the start of the incorrect period, I'd begin to undress, look around and see no familiar faces. I'd slam my wire basket back onto its shelf and race back up the stairs to the hallways, reaching behind my back to zip the awful orange dress as I ran.

On the right days, I was the last girl to leave my chlorinated sanctuary. I arrived at the next class late, hair dripping and eyes flaming red from the nitrates in the pool.

Although I'd gotten straight A's in sixth grade, homework was another foreign concept. I seldom carried any textbooks home. Without them I couldn't complete assignments or study for tests—which always came as a great surprise to me.

Mom never asked why I didn't have homework—after all, Dave didn't have any either.

My grades, formerly on an honor roll level, plummeted. By October of that year I began to suffer a terrifying nightmare where I begged students in the halls to help me find my next class. In the dream—as in reality—I didn't know my schedule. Without the security of having one classroom, one teacher, and one desk I felt wretched. Desperate, but awkward and shy, I'd approach kids in the crowds milling between classes and plead to them for help. "Do you know me? Am I in your next class?"

Trying to find my way through life's twists and turns, the same nightmare recurred many times over the next twenty years. The good thing about nightmares is that you eventually wake up when no one answers.

• • •

On Christmas Eve, Dad picked me up for our church's candlelight service. We passed houses where porch lights shone and Christmas trees blinked bright colors from behind their warm glass prisons. I hummed "Silent Night" and "O Little Town of Bethlehem," hoping Dad would join in. Instead of singing in his usual booming baritone, he remained silent and pushed hard on the accelerator, leaving the city behind. As the car climbed up the mountain at the edge of town, I sang louder, wanting him to hear me over the roaring motor.

Dad explained he was thinking about his music and asked me to be quiet. I didn't remember anything difficult from recent choir rehearsals but thought he'd planned to play a complex introit or offertory tonight. Since he didn't sing with me, I gave up and leaned against the cold window, mesmerized by the snow rushing into the headlights. As we drove over dark roads, the luminous white swirls flew onto the hood. I tried to pick a single flake but they came as one mass, disappearing on the glass, blotting out the night. The wipers swept the windshield clean, and I hunted another lone flake.

Dad eased into the small town and parked along the almost deserted main street near the church. I swung my door open wide, hoping to push back the snow bank clinging to the edge of the walk. The door's bottom edge scraped the curb, and the loud sound made me cringe. I looked across the top of the car for Dad's reaction, expecting some rebuke. He'd already closed his door and began hurrying across the slushy street.

"Wait, Daddy!" I skittered around the car's fender, rushed to his side, and grabbed his large, warm hand.

Dad looked down at me and smiled. That one quick smile made me so happy I wanted to skip through the glow of the streetlight. I was too old for skipping though, and to prove it to myself, I walked carefully so my boots wouldn't splash the dirty water onto Dad's trousers.

Stepping out of the cold into the vestibule, I stomped my feet on the mat. We'd arrived early to warm up the organ and practice a few minutes before the choir arrived. I leaned down to pull off my boots as Dad passed me and disappeared into the sanctuary.

I dismissed a shuffling noise, thinking it must be the church's old heater rumbling to life in the basement below. Unbuttoning my coat, I heard the unmistakable giggling of a child. Dripping black galoshes in hand, I straightened up, peering into the darkness of the narrow room.

Shocked, I found myself looking at someone I'd not seen in months—a soprano from Dad's former Episcopal church choir.

She wore a close-fitting navy coat, matching hat, and round-toed high heels. No ugly boots. Marianne stood there with her three young, fidgeting children, who didn't seem at all surprised to see me. Poking each other and grinning, they rushed at me. I came forward, holding my dripping boots behind my back. I'd babysat these children a number of times, and I hugged them with one arm and wished their mother a Merry Christmas.

I didn't stay and exchange pleasantries like an adult but headed downstairs to change into my choir robe.

From her seat in the front pew, Marianne beamed at me through the service. Once or twice, I turned around to look at my father, sitting high on his bench at the organ behind the choir. Looking over my head in Marianne's direction, he smiled too. Slender and tanned, she looked pretty in the candlelight. As we sang "Silent Night," I thought everybody sure seemed happy that Christmas.

In the afterglow of the last carol, church parishioners hugged one another and murmured subdued Merry Christmases. I passed a few of my own greetings to the choir and stepped into the night to catch up to Dad. I couldn't quite figure out why Marianne seemed to be heading to Dad's car with us. *Maybe she parked her car near ours.* She walked beside my father, smiling and talking low to him, while her children followed along behind.

Anxious for our car's heater to warm me, I hurried ahead through the falling snow. As I grasped the front door handle, she caught up, reached around me, and removed my hand.

"You ride in the back. Your father and I are married now."

The windshield wipers beat a steady rhythm as he drove. The snow crunched and squeaked beneath the tires. Pressing against the door, I tried to disappear as my mind swirled and eddied like snow-flakes the night's cold wind pushed back and forth.

Dad's silence seemed normal behavior of late.

I liked Marianne and always thought she was pretty. I liked her two little boys and adored her daughter. Last year she sometimes took me home after church and never failed to stop at a drugstore to buy me a Milky Way candy bar, which my father never allowed us to have at home.

Mulling through disturbing visions, I worried, how could Daddy love me *now*, with her in *my* seat in his car? Worse yet, Marianne was probably in the house Daddy and I shared all summer and fall. It remained quiet in the car all the way back to my mother's house. I was too young to contemplate my father and Marianne sharing a bed, or sweet baby Noel, born a year later.

Watching the car's tail lights disappear as they drove off, I felt left out and abandoned. Another childhood wound. Another well-learned lesson in hurting loved ones.

I turned toward my mother's house, crying as I trudged through the snow covering her winding slate walk. I could see light spilling from Mom's parted draperies upstairs. Through the living room windows, I saw she left the Christmas tree lights on for me, but the darkness inside my heart subdued their brightness.

Inside the green-paneled front door, I yanked off my boots and sent them scudding across the hallway into the corner. I slung my coat onto Mom's blue chair.

The Christmas tree and measly four packages beneath it looked forlorn. I unplugged the tree lights and turned off the dining room lamp before climbing the stairs. I dressed in pajamas and slippers and scuffed through the hallways to my momma's room. When I sat next to her, my throat pinched in a painful sting, and I began to cry again. I told Mom what had happened.

She put her book aside and pulled back the covers, inviting me to share her warm bed. Momma stroked my hair. "You have to be brave and hold your head up, no matter how much you cry inside. I know it hurts, honey. *I know.*"

. . .

I continued to see my dad, spending weekends at The Farm with him and his new bride, while her children visited their father five miles away.

Several years younger than Dad and inexperienced with preteen behavior, Marianne attempted to befriend her jealous new step-daughter. She tried to blend her three bewildered children with two of her new husband's much older, confused, and resentful ones. We all struggled through the weekends—Dad, Marianne, her three children, Dave, and me.

I didn't care for Marianne's unfamiliar cooking. I disliked anyone telling me to pick up my room, much less *her*. And I resented having no private time with my father in which just he and I sang. I extended my long horseback rides in the woods.

Dave hunted woodchucks at the farm on occasion but usually stayed in the city. When he did come, he didn't attempt to hide his smoking and displayed an open, hostile attitude toward Marianne. If she tried to help him with his schoolwork, he ignored her assistance.

I don't recall Dad scolding Dave's behavior, as he would most certainly have in the past. Instead, my father disregarded both my brother's insolence and his smoking habit. He worked his usual long hours, while his young wife struggled to develop our relationships.

Embarrassed by Dave's aggression, I felt sorry for both my mother and now Marianne, and I often worried whose purse his cigarette money came from.

Chapter Four

In the fall of 1959, I began ninth grade. Dave had joined the army and although our family had dwindled down to just Mom and me, we still treaded rough waters. Hearing she'd make good money in the winter hospitality industry, Mom decided she'd work the tourist season in Miami as a restaurant hostess.

We didn't get the newspaper. Mom didn't have time for television news. She didn't know about the massive influx of Cuban refugees fleeing Castro's rule. By the time she stepped off the bus, there were thousands of penniless, desperate Cuban families flooding the job markets of Miami. Willing to work long hours for very little pay, they took any employment available.

Mom answered help wanted ads for classy restaurants every day. She was attractive and well spoken, but young, beautiful Cuban girls trumped her. Broke, she took the first job she could find—as a chambermaid in a large hotel. While she struggled in her grueling job in Florida, I stayed with one of her best friends.

Annis lived a block from my high school in a quaint white house with black shutters. Her rooms sparkled, and a pleasant scent of lemon and bay floated about. I slept in a beautiful bedroom under a soft wool blanket and had an entire dresser all to myself. I luxuriated in my very own bathroom. I soaked in the tub, using scoopfuls of wonderful-smelling crystals from elegant jars. I lined Annis's pretty bath linens in neat rows on the towel racks. In the midst of this comforting order, it seemed easier to keep my clothes picked up and the bed made.

Annis cooked wonderful meals. We ate dinner seated in Windsor chairs at an old pine trestle table, worn and polished to a soft luster. I couldn't help but compare her matching pieces to those at home where nothing matched. Some evenings we sat by a cheery fire, reading in elegant chairs. Annis asked about my day, talked about the parents of some of my school friends, and hugged me as I went to bed. She never forgot to give me lunch money. Nevertheless, Annis wasn't Mom.

. . .

I still went to Dad's on the weekends. Concerned about my poor academic performance as much as Dave's, Marianne asked about assignments and encouraged me through dreaded math classes. She checked my homework and brought home library books for my English term paper weekend research on Mary, Queen of Scots. I spent hours reading, writing, and rewriting the paper to make it error and smudge free.

Anticipating a high mark for the first time since sixth grade, I waited while the teacher handed back our term papers. It seemed to take him forever to get to my row. With a somber look, rather than handing it to me, he placed my work face down and moved on to the next desk. I turned the paper over. A bright red F in the upper right corner leapt off the page.

Dumbfounded, I stared at it the rest of the period. He'd circled two or three punctuation errors, but I saw no other explanation except for red, double slashes beneath *abdicate* and the word "plagiarism" written in the margin.

Sobbing, I called Dad that night. While Annis stroked my heaving back, I gave him the story. He picked me up the next morning, made sure I had the offending paper with me, and for the first time in my life, drove me to school. Hand firm on my shoulder, he propelled me straight to the tall counter in the room most students avoided at all costs: the office. He spoke in a deep, strong voice. "We need to see the principal." Dad didn't seem the least bit nervous.

Two women busied themselves at their desks. Another disappeared into the principal's office. I heard the principal tell her to summon my English teacher. We didn't wait long.

Refusing a seat, Dad stood behind me as I sat staring into my lap. My father pushed my paper across the desk. "This project looks to me like it deserves praise, not a failing grade. I'd like your opinion, sir."

The silence broke only as the principal turned the pages while he read. My heart pounded so loud I felt certain he and Dad both heard it. I jumped when my teacher knocked as he came through the door. His eyes locked on me, then my father, then to the paper in front of us all. Frowning, he took a step toward the desk.

My face burned. I wanted to cry and crawl onto Daddy's lap. I did neither.

The principal held up his finger in a wait-a-minute gesture. He finished reading, laid the piece on the blotter, and motioned my teacher to a place beside his desk.

I kept my head ducked during introductions. Beside me, I watched my teacher's fingers fidget with his tweed jacket buttons, then slide into his gray trouser pocket. I heard the jingle of coins. The distinct odor of sweat sank over my face. I couldn't help myself and sniffed aloud. I looked up enough to see him push his heavy-framed, thick glasses into the hair stretching eyebrow to eyebrow above the bridge of his nose. I hated that too familiar motion—he seemed to adjust those glasses every five minutes during my English period.

The principal cleared his throat and leaned toward my teacher. "Mr. Granger would like an explanation of his daughter's grade on her term paper. I have to agree there seems little explanation for this failing mark." He folded his hands, nodded, waited.

In his usual whiny voice, teacher's words came out in a staccato rhythm, echoing around the walls. "It's obvious she copied parts of her paper out of an encyclopedia. The word *abdicate* is far beyond any ninth grader's vocabulary."

Dad spoke with eloquence as he defended my work as original, detailing how much time and effort I'd put into the paper. He surprised me with how much he knew about it—Marianne must have filled him in. He challenged the teacher. "Why don't you ask her a question about that period—or anything she might have researched?"

Braver now, I lifted my head in time to see my teacher narrow his eyes at me. "Okay. Donna, tell us what *abdicate* means."

The term had been used in every reference I'd read. My face flaming hot, I swallowed hard. "It meant Mary renounced her right to rule. She gave up the throne."

The principal told me to go to my next class.

Dad gave my shoulder a squeeze as I passed him. I wasn't sure why—maybe due to my slight sense of triumph—but without thinking about it, I knew the direction to the correct room.

I received an A on the term paper. That A gave me a sense of confidence for the first time in three years. With Marianne's gentle guidance and suggestions, I began to enjoy researching.

Pushing his glasses up into those bushy eyebrows, the teacher winked at me as he handed back my next English paper a few weeks later. It had numerous red corrections, and once again, the grade reflected none of my concentrated efforts.

Frustrated, I showed Annis the paper, and she suggested I call my father again. He seemed to take it even harder than me.

Dad called Mom in Florida, and the following week I moved to the farm with Dad and Marianne and began attending a much smaller Lake George High School. My grades rose to a more respectable level.

Sharing a house with young siblings gave me measles and strep throat. Fretting from pain and fever, I longed for my mother's touch and the coolness of her custard sliding down my fiery throat. In the shade-darkened room, I yearned to hear her voice telling me stories of her youth.

Jealousy aside, I emerged unscathed after a winter of living with two much younger stepbrothers, a stepsister, a baby half sister, and a father infatuated with his wife.

• • •

Mom finished her work in Florida at the end of tourist season. She'd been gone almost four months, and I'd missed her every single day. I couldn't wait to see her and for us both to get back home again.

She suggested it would be wonderful if Dad would send me to meet her in New York City. We'd stay on Long Island with her friend Barbara, whose daughter once owned the hated orange dress. She told him to pack me nice clothes as she planned to celebrate our reunion by taking me to see a Broadway show. Dad bought me a bus ticket; Marianne bought me new clothes for the trip.

I felt excited and grown up but also frightened at taking a two hundred–mile trip alone. I boarded the bus for the long trip from Glens Falls to New York City. People around me dozed in between stops on the five-hour journey. I stared out the window, daydreaming about how happy my momma would be to see me again.

Buses and people hurrying in every direction crowded the loud, fume-filled Port Authority Terminal. After I retrieved my suitcase from the baggage area underneath the bus and followed other passengers inside, I found my way to the information booth.

People jostled me from every direction, but I stood my ground. I scanned the throngs of people, anxious to find my mother. After several moments of fearing she wasn't there, I spied my pretty mother.

She looked straight past me as she talked with Barbara. I hurried over, expecting a long hug. Momma kept on talking—ignoring me. Deflated and close to tears, I dropped my faux leather suitcase by her feet. "Aren't you even going to say hello?"

Startled, Mom took a step back as she looked at me. Barbara stared. My face grew hot, and my throat seemed to close. Our small circle stayed silent. After an interminable moment my mother laughed, pulled me close, and reached up to give me the embrace I longed for.

I'd lost weight from the strep throat, grown four inches taller in her absence, and now wore glasses. In new red high heels, I towered above my mother. My naturally curly hair frizzed into a mass, thanks to my first home permanent. I carried a purse, wore a dressy red straw hat, red gloves, and a new navy coat. It was no wonder Momma didn't recognize her own daughter.

We took a train to Long Island. In Barbara's car, Momma spoke of her Florida experiences. "I sure didn't make much down there, even though I worked as many hours as my boss would let me. I was so tired I could barely eat, but I couldn't sleep when I went to my room. I worried about everything—the money, bills, and how Donna was doing."

Despite the fact I was too old for such behavior, I hung against the back of the front seat, my long arms draped about my mother's shoulders. I couldn't stop touching her. Momma had changed in Florida. For one thing, she no longer laughed with the hearty, deep chuckle I'd heard so often in our past. I could see she'd lost weight, and her tanned skin glowed next to my winter pallor. Her auburn hair, cut in a short, sophisticated style, sparkled with new silver strands.

After we reached Barbara's house, we sat at the kitchen table for tea. Momma talked nonstop. When Barbara filled our cups, I watched Mom's hand shake as she reached for hers. Then I realized her head shook as well.

Momma told us that the third time she'd fainted at work her boss dropped her off at an emergency room. A harried resident flipped through her chart, glanced over the nurse's notes, and verified the blood pressure readings. He rattled off a few questions and scribbled Mom's answers.

Telling us about it, her eyes welled with tears. "When he asked about my family, I cried. I don't know what happened. When he called me '*Mrs.* Granger,' I asked, 'Please just call me Eleanor.' I told him how tired I was after long hours on a thankless job. I told him how I hated working with people who chattered all day in another language. Chambermaids were assigned rooms in teams, and I tried to be friendly to the Cuban women, but none of them would help me with my rooms.

"I couldn't seem to earn enough money to make any difference in our lives." Mom turned in her seat to look back at me, "And I missed you so much, honey."

The doctor advised her to quit her job. "The best thing you can do is to go home. Find another way to make a living. You can't let your blood pressure get this high again. As it is, you're going to need medication for the rest of your life." He shook her hand and added, "You know, Eleanor, somehow, I get the feeling you're going to be all right."

• • •

When Mom and I arrived back in Glens Falls, it was about one o'clock in the afternoon. Walking home from the bus station, I imagined she'd make us cucumber sandwiches and a cup of tea. We'd laugh and share stories, dawdle over the dishes.

To my surprise, Mom went right upstairs to her bedroom. I followed her and lingered by the side of her bed, still hungry for the sight of my mother. She stepped out of her dress and shoes and peeled off her nylons, left on her pretty beige half slip. She drew the draperies, and crawled under the quilt on her bed.

She looked around the room with a slight smile on her lips, yawned, and said, "Every woman should wake up in a pink bedroom." In an instant, Momma closed her blue eyes and began a soft snuffling breathing that told me she'd gone to sleep. She slept and slept.

I cooked meatloaf, baked potatoes, and corn pudding for dinner. I made certain she could hear me banging around in the kitchen.

As the dinner baked, I knew it scented the whole house—I sniffed outside her room to make sure of that too.

Mom didn't come downstairs.

Several times that evening I checked to see if she was awake. Before going to bed, I wrapped her plate in wax paper and put it in the refrigerator. Around eight the next morning, I shook her shoulder. "Momma, are you ready for breakfast?"

A few hours later, I asked about lunch. Both times, she told me she just wanted to sleep. I worried because I didn't know what else to do.

As it began to grow dark, the woman who would thereafter inspire my spirit with her indomitable will to live life to its fullest came downstairs. She'd showered and washed her hair. Her skin smelled of her favorite yellow Jean Naté after-bath lotion. Momma looked young, confident, and never more beautiful as she swept into the kitchen in a long waist-hugging smoke blue and white polka dotted robe. *She's even prettier than Loretta Young.*

My mother looked so good *I* felt pretty.

Wrapping her arm around my waist, Mom picked up her food-splattered 1932 cookbook. "Let's make bread pudding." While my mother buttered slices of bread and cut them into large squares, I grated the Baker's semi-sweet chocolate bar and toasted the nuts. Momma beat the devil out of the eggs, added milk, sugar, and vanilla. Chocolate-topped bread pudding had always been one of our favorite desserts, but that one was the best ever. To have my mother home and in charge again felt real good.

We slipped back into familiar routines. That summer I took driver's education, learned the basics of becoming a good waitress at a small diner, and cleaned a funeral home three mornings a week.

My mother worked at a more glamorous job, as hostess for a popular restaurant. She wore tailored suits, beautiful dresses, and high heels—most of which were from her days in the dress shop. She no longer appeared as a dispirited divorcee, but I knew when she felt insecure. Despite putting up a good front, her hands, head, and voice—steady or quaking—revealed how nervous she felt.

At a checkup, as Mom's doctor refilled her blood pressure pill prescription, he asked about her tremors. Obvious to everyone except my mother, her head now shook constantly.

"Oh, you mean my hands," Mom asked.

"Well, yes, and your head shakes. Does it get worse when you're tired?"

"Oh, my," she said, "I didn't know my head shook."

He diagnosed it as a benign old age tremor, adding, "That's what Katherine Hepburn has, you know."

Mom came home and told me she had a very famous "shake."

Chapter Five

Tenth grade began. On a social level, I found high school a bit easier than junior high's tumultuous years. I made new friends, fell in love with Elvis Presley, and developed crushes on more available guys. I spent weekend days playing 45-RPM records with my two best friends, and Friday and Saturday nights dancing at our Teen Canteen.

Although I always loved being with him, I saw less of my father on weekends as I stumbled through our evolving relationship. When Dad went home from work, he wanted to relax with his young family but often encouraged me to visit. "Why don't you come up this weekend, honey? We'll have a picnic and go swimming one last time before it gets too cold."

Thoughts of swimming with Dad swirled as I remembered how he'd once encouraged me as a little girl to swim farther, faster, better.

• • •

Just before my sixth birthday, after much practice, I announced I wanted to swim across the bay. I knew there could be no putting my feet down: Dad and I had disposed of a leaky sailboat, mast and all, in the middle of this bay. I'd watched in perverse delight as my father chopped a hole in its center and it sank. Although we could see a great distance down into the dark emerald water, neither boat nor mast was visible.

My father rowed a few feet ahead, encouraging me, ready to pull me into the boat if I became too tired to continue. My stroke faltered, and I spluttered when waves from distant boats washed over me, but I wouldn't give up. My arms, feeling weighted by lead sinkers, splashed in front of my head. Feeble kicks barely propelled me toward the massive rock that beckoned me for the half hour crossing. Searching for the lake bottom, I stretched my leg below repeatedly. I almost sank as the last of my energy dissipated when my toes brushed slimy rocks. The next solid step brought me to shoulder-depth water. I staggered up the mossy slope of Joshua's Rock.

With long screeches and scraping sounds, Daddy beached the boat, stepped over its side, and scooped me from waist-deep water. I clung to his strong shoulders as he knelt, wrapped me up tight in my favorite pink towel, and rubbed my aching arms and quivering legs. I didn't mind he rubbed so hard the friction felt like the "nuggies" my brother Dave inflicted on me with his knuckles. His breath tickled as he whispered, "My brave little Donna."

For a while, we sat together listening to the hypnotic sounds of waves lapping against the rock. It was difficult to say if it was the sun-warmed towel, his strong arm around my shoulders, or my father's smiling expression of pride that heated me that afternoon.

• • •

By late fall, Dad practically had to beg me to visit. I enjoyed riding my horse, but he made it clear he wouldn't pick me up, have me stay long enough only to ride, then drive me home again. He still worked Saturday mornings and wasn't home until late afternoon. The farm was not only nine miles away from Glens Falls but also three miles from the lake. Dad no longer owned the cottage, of course, so he had to rent a stall at a marina for his boat. Swimming wasn't just pulling on a bathing suit and jumping off our dock into the water. It now included packing the car with towels, picnic supplies, and all the other paraphernalia necessary for his growing family of five children.

I made excuses and lied about weekend school commitments. I didn't want to hurt his feelings by telling him I felt marooned at the farm. I didn't explain that I wanted to be with my friends and close enough to walk to the movies, an ice cream soda shop, or to the canteen.

I continued to sing in choir and rode to church with Dad for Wednesday evening practice and Sunday services. Since I seldom cared for or even rode my horse, Dad sold it. Because I didn't visit often, I found out weeks after the fact. Clinging to the belief my father wouldn't do such a thing, I blamed Marianne. I refused to see my part in his decision. I cried about losing my horse and the sense of escape I enjoyed when I rode. Fifteen-year-old self-importance chafed with helplessness and frustration at the additional commotion in my life.

Religion didn't mean much to me. "Church" was a beautiful building where I spent a few hours a week singing with Dad. As morning sunshine poured through the stained glass windows over the choir, I daydreamed rather than listened to the lesson. I memorized anthems written with love and joy by the likes of Mendelssohn and Bach, but I didn't embrace their messages either.

• • •

After school, popular kids spent time at the soda fountain downtown. I longed to be there too, listening to the jukebox, expounding on which boy was the cutest, but I couldn't afford to go. I couldn't tell my friends there was no point in asking for a quarter for three songs or a Pepsi, much less a chocolate soda. I felt miserable and moped about until Mom's sage advice smoothed our precarious financial situation.

"Just keep smiling, honey. Use your manners, find something kind to do for someone else, and you'll feel better inside."

I wrestled with the task of finding something "kind" but not too challenging. A few days later, an idea came when I heard the lady across the street lean out her upstairs window and call for her cat.

"Mittens! Meat, Mittens, meat." I watched the large tabby hop into a wicker basket sitting on the ground and sit perfectly still as the basket was hauled upwards by means of a long rope. At the open second-story window, a thin hand steadied the basket while the cat jumped across the sill and disappeared inside. Seconds later, the window slammed shut.

The cat's owner, Mrs. D., had always carried a certain mystique. The sight of her stooped back, wispy white hair, and sharp features mesmerized me as a child. Her raspy voice and harsh tone frightened me. I used to spy on her from beneath our forsythia bush, and although terrified she'd come over and "get" me if she joined her cat in her small front yard, I mimicked her calls to Mittens. While I ate supper at our kitchen table, I often watched her witchlike profile in an upstairs window across the street.

She seldom came outdoors now, and because I was older, she didn't seem quite as scary. I thought I might help with the cat—maybe play with him, give him a saucer of milk on occasion. I could tell my friends I had a demanding after-school job.

Feeling rather virtuous, I explained these noble thoughts to my mother. Mom said, "I think that'd be very nice." She went on to tell me our neighbor was quite elderly now and that her eyesight had failed to the point of near blindness.

A blind lady? Uh, oh. Maybe this wasn't such a good idea.

Mom sent me right across the street.

I stepped into a dark foyer, punctuated by a staircase and banister. I looked up, calling, "Hello," as I climbed the steep stairs. No answer. A single bulb hung from a black cord above the top landing. "Hello?" The bulb flickered with each of my steps. Still no answer.

I reached the top step and knocked on the door. I knew she was inside, but my idea no longer felt good. I knocked as loud as I dared, giving myself one last chance at nobility.

Okay, one more time, and I can just tell Mom she moved or something.

I raised my hand, knuckles poised inches from the wood.

The door flew open.

An old woman squinted through glasses with lenses thick as Coke bottles as she leaned through the gap and came close to my face.

I backed up several steps, gripping the top of the banister to keep from going over backward.

"Who's there?"

Amid "It's Donna—Eleanor's daughter... from across the street," and many more "Who's there?" questions I stumbled even farther back toward the stairwell's abyss.

Mom neglected to mention Mrs. D. couldn't hear a freight train at her door. I saw my shadow crouching on the wall beside me and wondered if I could beat it down to the door.

I wasn't certain if the old hag understood me, but she finally stepped back and said, "Well come on in here. Why didn't you tell me who you were? Sit here where I can see you."

I'd encountered the wolf in Red Riding Hood's grandmother's bed. I backed into a chair and watched speckles of dirt rise around me.

"Do you like to read?"

"Yes."

"Speak up. I can't hear you!"

"Yes!"

"Good." That apparently settled and clarified everything. The old woman lit a Camel cigarette held between two yellowed fingers, hacked, and spewed forth a half-hour of loud monologue on her favorite books and authors.

Dirt smudged her thick glasses. Dried bits of spittle caked the corners of her mouth, and long black hairs jutted from her chin. An oversized black cardigan, stained man's dress shirt, and gray wool trousers hung in shapeless bags around her gaunt body. Her stockings drooped from beneath her pant legs in sagging folds over the top of her black sturdy shoes.

Still, there was something engaging about this lady. In between fits of loud, awful coughing, I discovered Mrs. D. was a retired English professor. Writers whose names I connected only with book titles came alive through her raspy voice. I heard how they lived, where they wrote, and whether fame shone on them before they died or afterward. She often didn't hear well enough to decipher my questions and waved a knobby hand to silence me.

Adding to the cigarette smoke, a distinct musty odor pervaded my space as I settled back into the brown leather with cracks criss-crossing its surface. Listening, trying to move as little as possible to still the dust and ignore the smells, I took in the grimy apartment. Crumbled papers littered the floor about her desk and the wastebasket overflowed. Dust covered her typewriter, and the cap on her ink-bottle had been screwed on crooked. Through a narrow doorway, I saw dishes stacked precariously close to the edge of the drain board.

I never mentioned Mittens that afternoon. He paid us no attention as he sat on the windowsill, licking a white paw and rubbing it over his striped face.

Still, as my goal was to help with the cat, I ventured back across the street two days later. Same result. I received plenty of literature instruction but no questioning of my sudden interest.

On the third visit, contents of the overturned wastebasket littered the floor. I wondered if Mittens had been busy or if the old woman had kicked it over. I asked if she minded my emptying it on my way out.

"It's not necessary. In fact, I'd rather you didn't."

Pressing on, I asked, "Then, could I just straighten up the kitchen a little?"

"No. Everything's just fine in there."

An aisle formed by stacks of newspapers led to the bathroom. One afternoon, I found the arm of a sweater trailing into the center of this walkway. Worried she'd trip and fall, I plucked the sweater off the chair arm and hung it in a closet.

"Just what do you think you're doing, young lady?" Mrs. D's thundering voice startled me.

"Well, I just wanted to pick up your sweat—"

"You mean, you wanted to put it where I'd never find it again?"

"No, I was just trying to help. The sleeve was right in the middle, and you could have fallen, and I thought…"

"Get out of here! I don't need you hiding my things."

I fled down the steep stairs to the dark hallway below and slammed the door. I raced across the street to my house and whined the whole story to my mother. How I'd tried to do something nice for someone. In fact, I'd tried hard to be useful and helpful several times. How I thought I could help an old woman who was gruff and mean to me.

Momma set me straight.

"Honey, she can't see! She's probably frightened out of her wits. That little apartment is her whole world now, and she finds things by leaving them where she can touch them. That's why she doesn't want you to clean up."

Mom and I baked banana bread and took it across the street the next Saturday. In a voice much louder than I could ever manage, Momma told her I wanted to help by cleaning a little. "It'd be good for Donna, and you won't have to worry about her picking up things you don't want disturbed. She promises she'll ask where you want something before she puts anything in a cupboard or closet, okay?"

Then we all bawled. Before Mom and I left, I told Mrs. D. exactly where the banana bread sat in her refrigerator.

From then on, while I swept her kitchen and cleaned the tiny bathroom, I learned about authors, poets, and famous ivy-covered universities Mom and I could never hope to afford. I made sure Mittens had fresh water, that the quart of milk in the refrigerator hadn't spoiled, and that the bread wasn't moldy. From the trash, the refrigerator and the cupboard, I learned what Mrs. D. ate. Not much, it seemed. Before long, I began to print a grocery list in huge block letters and leave it by the telephone. After school on Tuesdays, I crossed the street to find a box of groceries waiting in the foyer. I carried them up to the apartment and put them away.

After I cleaned on Saturday mornings, the old woman reached into a jar for my pay. I quietly returned each quarter to the jar and smiled all the way down her stairs. Chocolate sodas didn't seem important anymore.

Chapter Six

One May evening more than four years after my parents' divorce, Mom answered the phone in the den. I could tell by her side of the conversation something good was happening. I flopped on the daybed and pretended to read *Auntie Mame*. Mom sat at her desk, doodling on the soft green blotter. "Yes, I can come then. Sure, I'm comfortable with that. No, I don't drive—she'd need to arrange a carpool."

At last, she replaced the black receiver in its cradle. Curious, I watched as she absently twirled the dial with her pencil a few times and then wrote two dates on the blotter. She took the Norman Rockwell calendar down from the wall and flipped ahead a page. "I'm going to work out of town in June."

I still remembered her last absence. I flung my book aside and sat up. "What do you mean, Mom? You're not going to Florida again, are you?"

In a deliberate, carefree voice, Mom explained that a woman from Long Island had hired her to care for a daughter-in-law expecting her third child. By now, she had a healthy self-confidence in her innate abilities. An excellent cook, she loved children and had a variety of domestic skills. Mom agreed to care for this young family through the mother's stay in the hospital and afterward until she was back on her feet.

"You'll only have two more weeks of school left, so while I'm away, you're old enough to stay by yourself, right, honey? I mean, well..." She extended a bare foot and wiggled her toes. "You know how much my feet hurt from standing in heels all night. I'll make much better money doing this."

I knew her feet hurt. I knew we needed the money. The more I thought about it, the better it sounded. The prospect of the house all to myself thrilled me. I'd stay up late, buy whatever sounded good at the new supermarket down the block, and play records as loud as I wanted.

Mom's hand shook as she pushed the calendar back onto the nail on the wall. I watched her lips move as she counted the days again. "Dale will come by to check on you." She had a weak little smile as she turned back to me. "Long distance is expensive, but I'll call as often as I can." She brightened a little more. "You can always call your father if you need anything."

Reality hit the first night. While proud Mom felt I was mature enough to stay at home by myself, being alone frightened me. I left lights burning in the living room and upstairs hall when I went to bed. The quiet house of daytime creaked and groaned in the dark. Nighttime wrapped me in lonely hours. I slept in Mom's bed so I could be near the upstairs phone in case she called.

Mom delighted her new employers so much they referred my mother to relatives and friends. She booked several jobs for the summer and into fall. Her new career involved much more than babysitting. Children left in her care astonished their happy parents by making their own beds, putting away toys, and going to bed with no argument. Mothers found handmade dresses for their little girls and witnessed picky-eater sons gobbling down vegetables during "Mrs. G's" fabulous story-hour at dinnertime.

Mom told me she always answered with a smile when parents asked, "How'd you get our kids to do that?"

"Big motivators: realistic expectations, frequent praise, and great desserts."

She insisted employers arrange carpools while she worked at their homes. She often laughed as she asked me, "Can you imagine me driving the Long Island Expressway while giggling seven-year-olds gave directions to their Brownie meeting?"

She stayed with her temporary families until their newborns slept through the night—usually for three or four weeks. Mom bonded easily with these young women. As their husbands advanced up corporate ladders, Mother sampled luxurious lifestyles in dozens of cities. Word of "our Eleanor" spread through women's circles from the Hamptons to Palo Alto. It sounded all very glamorous, but in actuality, she worked very hard.

It wasn't long before coming home to an empty dark house was hard for me too. Locking the front door and hurrying upstairs, I snuggled deep into the security of my mother's bed and read late into the night. Yearning for the sound of her voice, I lived for the nights she would call. I cried myself to sleep many of the nights in between her calls.

. . .

Because of her new work, we had more income, but we both struggled to manage our household funds. We still couldn't afford a dentist except for emergencies, but with the help of her new work, the grocery budget increased. We paid our accounts with the dry cleaner, the department store, and the drugstore on time.

Approaching our driveway one afternoon, the whine of a saw came from the back yard. I rounded the corner of the house and saw a tall man dressed in overalls bent over two sawhorses. Sawdust spewed across the grass. Calm as you please, Mom sat in a chair by the porch, facing the stranger. Two glasses with melting ice shimmered in the warm sunshine near a sweating pitcher of iced tea. Two plates with crumbs and a bread crust rested on a small tray table.

Mom saw me first, scooted to the side of the chair, and patted the empty space, inviting me to join her. "Honey, this is Bernie. He's working on a big surprise for you." Beaming, she leaned toward me. "I've saved enough money so we can have a little help around here. Bernie is a handyman."

The man turned, looked at Mom, and grinned. His arms glistened with sweat and a fine covering of sawdust stuck to the golden hairs of his muscled forearms.

"Bernie, come meet my daughter Donna."

Bernie strode across the lawn toward us, brushing his hands off against his pant legs. The closer he got to me, the larger he loomed. I kept my eyes on his work boots, spattered with thick flecks of white material. The boots stopped inches from my mother's chair. "She's even prettier than you said, Ellie."

Ellie? No one called my mom that—unless he was a good friend. How could that be? His nearness to my mother somehow embarrassed me. I watched her smile at him and realized she wore lipstick. In the middle of the day.

"Pleased ta meet ya, Donna. How ya doin'?"

I mumbled "hello," backed toward the screen door, and fled to the sanctuary of the kitchen. I turned the faucet on full force until the water turned cold. I splashed it on my burning face, not caring that water ran off my arms onto the floor. I heard my mother's laughter and a deep voice. I retraced a few steps back across the kitchen. I wanted to hear what Mom thought was so hilarious. I needed to know more about this Bernie.

Dad needed to know about this Bernie. No, that wasn't true. Dad didn't have the right to know anything about my mother.

Two low upstairs windows overlooked our back yard. I crept out of the kitchen, past the dining room table, toward the staircase. I noticed bits of sawdust on the runner and paused in uncertainty at the top of the stairs, looking down the hallway. My mattress sagged against the far wall, a pile of folded bedding sat on the dresser shoved face-first into the corner. Sawdust covered the floor and huge footprints mixed there with ones the size of Mom's shoes.

A row of new two by fours divided the bedroom Dad had creaked through on his way to surprise me as a little girl.

• • •

Saturday nights meant bath time. As I raced to my room afterward, I tugged a clothesline-fresh-smelling nightie over my damp body. Mommy perched on the end of my bed, and we waited, giggling, while Daddy slowly climbed the creaking stairs. By the sounds of the floorboards, I traced his progress through the big center bedroom into the hallway outside my room. Keeping to our script but somehow still always a bit startled, Mommy and I both jumped when he stuck his grinning face around the doorjamb. Daddy's shoulders seemed to fill my tiny room.

He leaned over the bed, pushed back the curls plastered to my forehead, and gave me a soft good night kiss. Completing the ritual, as he turned out the lamp Dad said, "Good night, my little chickadee."

My sage green youth bed creaked as Mom leaned over me and tucked me in tight.

Sleepy and relaxed from the warm bath water, I closed my eyes and murmured, "Tell him, Mommy. I'm his nurse, not his chickadee."

• • •

Masking tape held a scrap of paper to the wall. Mom's unmistakable shaky script read, "Sweet Dreams in Your New Bedroom!" As I studied the room, a sense of partition emerged—the studs formed a hallway and a generous new bedroom. I stepped through a wide doorway and headed to two short walls and a smaller opening. I had my very own closet.

Bernie hung sheetrock, mudded and sanded the seams, fixed the spring on our garage door, and built a large screened-in porch for Mom. In time, I got used to his generous smile and familiar ease. I tolerated his enthusiastic hugs, and relaxed when he gave one to my mother, provided it didn't last longer than I felt necessary. Whether the money, the projects, or the friendship ran out, I never knew, but several months later Bernie quit coming to our house.

I loved my new bedroom and asked to decorate it. We bought bright, white paint to coat the ceiling. I visited the hardware store every Saturday, going over giant wallpaper books until I found a small floral print.

When there was enough cash, Mom ordered my wallpaper. She had hung paper in almost every room in our old house, despite the challenges of its uneven horsehair plastered walls. The outside walls of my room curved up to meet the ceiling at a poorly defined angle, making it difficult to mark where to stop papering. Pushing my end of the heavy six-foot-long straight edge against the freshly painted ceiling, I chattered away as I drew the carpenter's pencil along its length.

Mother shrieked, "Stop!"

I froze, half-scared to death.

"Look what you've done!"

I followed her trembling arm as she pointed to the end of my pencil. I'd allowed the thick black line to drift far out onto the white ceiling.

Although most nights Mom and I read in our rooms before going to sleep, every so often she'd slide into the empty twin bed in my room. Listening to the red radio I'd received for my seventeenth birthday, we'd read or talk about her latest date. With magazines from a rummage sale propped open in front of us one night, I saw hers slip to reveal a dog-eared paperback inside.

Laughing, I held mine aloft from behind the *Ladies Home Journal.* We were both reading well-marked copies of *Lady Chatterley's Lover.*

• • •

Dad's musical tutelage came into play as I auditioned for the high school octet in the fall of my junior year. I waited in a long line of joking, jostling, anxious students. When the director called my name, I wasn't nervous.

Until he told me to read the second alto part, "A cappella, please."

The choir's accompanist slid from the piano bench. He blew one note on his pitch pipe.

I stood behind the empty bench, squinting at the unfamiliar music resting against the music rack. Drawing in a tremulous breath, I could hear my father, "Focus on the notes and your diction." It must have worked, because midway through the piece, the choir director stopped me.

"Class, I believe this young lady has perfect pitch!"

He added my name to the posted list of 1960-61 octet members.

I dipped into my precious savings to buy the required red wool blazer for our performances. We had to dress up when we sang at nighttime social outings, so I borrowed my mother's best dresses and high heels. Scottish to the core, Mom always hunted the newest styles in bargain basements of ritzy downtown department stores. I felt well dressed for the first time in years. Octet performances gave me enough self-confidence to win a role in a school play.

I didn't mind that neither of my parents ever heard me sing while in octet. My mother still didn't drive, and Dad had a growing new family. Nevertheless, I was proud of myself for belonging to such a prestigious group and sang aloud walking home at night after events. On a couple of occasions, two popular seniors gave me a ride home. Dressed in nice clothes, sitting between two handsome guys, I felt very special.

• • •

As Mom became a much-sought nanny, my culinary skills evolved. I followed recipes from her now coverless old cookbook. I developed a lifelong passion for cooking, priding myself on being able to make something delicious out of "nothing."

I worked after school, babysitting for my brother Dale and his wife, Anne. Despite my mother sometimes working out of town, I had a mature steady boyfriend—conscientious or Catholic enough never to let things get out of hand. He bought me an old car, enabling me to spend two long summers cleaning rooms in a Lake George motel. On our dates, we picked up fifteen-cent McDonald's hamburgers, went water skiing, then to the drive-in.

When the ancient car could no longer be repaired, my boyfriend came through again and bought me another old car for ten dollars. This one looked pretty snazzy, but I had to be very careful where I parked because it had no reverse gear. That summer I earned generous tips waitressing in a busy Lake George diner.

I saved every penny I could for nursing school.

• • •

I never doubted I'd be a nurse when I grew up. As a four-year-old, I'd sit on the slippery leather arm of my dad's chair, listen to his heart with my plastic stethoscope, and "fix" broken bones with a variety of inventive rag bandages. Sadly, even as a senior, I still wasn't a serious student. I had no real idea how to study but somehow managed to do well in a few subjects. Although my grades didn't reflect it, I maintained a steely resolve to become a nurse.

Mrs. Lamb, a compassionate guidance counselor, probed about my home life as she helped me fill out the single application form I'd requested for nursing school. Once she understood college tuition stood far beyond my limited savings, she didn't push me to apply elsewhere. When I received a polite letter of rejection, Mrs. Lamb intervened, persevering with the admissions committee, insisting I could and would succeed.

Chapter Seven

On a sunny Sunday afternoon in September 1962, amid crushes of excited, chattering other girls, luggage, hair dryers, and radios, I rode the elevator up to the third floor until all my belongings were in my dorm room. In the lobby, I snuffled a teary good-bye into my boyfriend's shirt and joined forty-four other freshman students entering a hospital-based Albany nursing school. That evening, we posed in clusters wearing our new uniforms. Because three-year programs were a work-study process in which students staffed the teaching hospital, my entire three-year tuition, books, and uniforms cost $427. Hard earned, it was the best money I ever invested.

A few weeks later, Dad drove me back to Albany after a weekend at home. My Grandma Granger asked to ride along, to see where I would spend the next three years of study. Together, we rode the elevator up to the freshman floor. Our dorm was brand new, and the bright, cheery rooms pleased her. She beamed from my desk chair as fellow students stopped by. Their incessant chatter about the past weekend, boyfriends, and home-cooked meals made her laugh with delight.

As I helped her into Dad's car, I couldn't help noticing her thinning hair. I gave her a long kiss on the cheek. Her breaths came in shallow gasps, but she smiled at me through the open window. "I'm so proud of you, honey. I know this is what you've wanted for a long time."

I stood, waving as Dad turned the car down the circle driveway and crossed into the northbound lane.

Grandma died two days later. Although I knew she was happy for me, I hated hearing that her doctor said the trip had been too much for her heart.

I returned to school after her funeral and found a note from Grandma in my mailbox. She'd written it the evening after seeing my school. I kept my grandmother's note in my desk drawer as a reminder that I was fulfilling her dream for me as well as my own.

• • •

Nursing school meant regimens and strict rules. Blue pinstriped uniforms with starched white aprons flowed down our white-stockinged legs, extending well past our knees. Nursing shoes, polished scuff-free, touted pristine laces. Whether giving a bed bath to a mannequin, making notes on his chart, or making the bed with precise corners and a smooth surface, students learned we couldn't ignore even the tiniest detail. In between clinical sessions, classes of chemistry, anatomy, and pharmacology filled our days.

Occasional laughter in the kitchenette where we gathered to do laundry drew us like a magnet. The laughter signaled someone recounting her experience with a patient, an instructor, or a physician. The louder the hooting, the more often students caved in and abandoned homework to share cups of cocoa or coffee.

Our freshman class was small, and living together through the newness of life away from home, we quickly developed into a tight group. I came out of my shell enough to regale my new friends with an account of giving my first full bed bath. I was the only student assigned a male patient. And not just any man, either.

My patient was a handsome twenty-year-old, confined to bed rest in a solarium room with three other men. The story of my red face, his embarrassment at having me as his nurse after having surgery on his backside to open and drain a cyst, and his roommates' comments had my colleagues collapsed in laughter. I'd found a niche telling stories and became a leader of sorts.

Each week began with two social privileges—twelve o'clock "late leaves" for Friday and Saturday nights. On all other nights our curfew was ten o'clock. As freshmen, we often endured bed checks by the housemother whose apartment was on our floor. Despite our restrictive deadlines, weekend evenings brought a steady parade of area college boys anxious to date student nurses, as well as a few boyfriends from home. Under the watchful eye of the housemother at the front desk, they waited in the lobby for us to step off the elevator and sign out for a dance or movie.

I had more than the usual share of visits with the nursing school director. At first, curfew violations were the cause. However, numerous pranks landed me in her office as well. I locked the ten stall doors in the bathroom and then slid out beneath them. Grumbling aloud with everyone else, I secretly thought it hilarious the next morning as forty-five of us lined up and used the first stall opened. I applied Vaseline to all our room door handles one afternoon, and another time covered the toilet bowls beneath the seats with plastic wrap.

For many weeks, Tuesdays seldom passed without these attention-seeking shenanigans causing me to lose my twelve o'clock privileges. Eager to show off, I led two much more dangerous pranks, which most certainly would have caused me and several other students an immediate dismissal from school. I helped a classmate re-enter the building after sneaking out after bed check to see her boyfriend until two a.m. On another occasion, I attempted to make the sprinkler system come on. Fortunately, I ran out of matches before I ruined our new building.

I was having the time of my life, dancing in my own little spotlight. The seriousness of my offenses didn't dawn on me until months later. Due to the school director's patience, encouragement to do better, and leniency as I matured, I gained self-esteem. I managed to have fun through it all but finally grew out of being the class clown.

My boyfriend tired of the one hundred-mile round trip to see me. I met other young men and dated as often as work schedules allowed.

I learned through many late-night discussions that while on dates, my peers and I maintained the same standards. We were all fun-loving, flirty, and "wild" enough to have one or two beers. We enjoyed dancing close enough to stir physical warmth. We sighed over cups of cocoa about how we desired to have someone we cared for enough to make out with on the way back to the dorm. But, always in the end, regardless of the groping and clinging, we remained chaste.

• • •

Even through studying tedious procedures, compassion came easily to me. I loved the time I spent on the wards, taking care of patients. I brushed angry tears as I bathed "Tom" one morning. Paralyzed from a stroke, Tom filled his hospital bed from end to end and side to side. His white, crew cut hair reeked, and he needed a shave. As a classmate helped me turn him on his side, the stench of his body and sweaty sheets gagged us both.

After making notes on his chart in the nurses' station, I returned to Tom's room for a quick check on him before I returned to classes. I met his wife, Mary, sitting in a chair by his bedside. "How does he look?" she asked.

He looked about the same, unless you counted the clean gown and sheets. I knew he smelled better, but I thought her question perplexing. Was she expecting a big change? While I formulated an answer, Mary explained she was blind. I vowed to come back that evening to do things time didn't allow on my day shift.

I returned to Tom's room after supper. Tom followed me with worried eyes, the only part of his body he could move. I stood over him with a disposable razor. "Don't worry, now, Tom. I've done this hundreds of times." I didn't fret about the lie—I'd never shaved a man in my life. I just hoped I wouldn't cut off his nose.

Exulted at only two small nicks on his chin, I propped his shoulders up with two pillows and let his head hang back over their edge. I slid a rubber half sheet under his head, applied a generous amount of shampoo, and scrubbed his head until his scalp gleamed pink through the suds.

I rotated off Tom's floor the next day but found him weeks later in the rehab department, shuffling along in a walker. An aide held a wide canvas belt around his middle. He smiled a lop-sided grin at me as I touched his hand on the walker.

I wanted to congratulate him on his progress. "I'm not sure you remember me, but I took care of you on the fourth floor. You're looking great!"

His head nodded up and down. He swallowed then spoke in a slow, halting monotone. "I'll never for..." He swallowed and tried again, "...forget that shave."

● ● ●

Two areas of nursing frightened me—labor and delivery and surgery. Being alone with a woman in labor terrified me. I fainted in surgery and spent more time in the recovery room than my patients did.

As part of our women's diseases course, I spent a day in a busy gynecologist's office. Intimidated by his bustling, efficient nurse, I followed her like a lost sheep looking for its momma. I didn't want to sound stupid, so I never asked a single question all morning. At lunchtime, I overheard the physician say, "She obviously isn't the least bit interested in office nursing—go ahead and send her back to school." Too humiliated to protest, I left the office, not having learned much at all.

By year two of nursing school, referred to as our junior year, each student took charge of thirty patients. Our organizational skills complemented the nursing expertise developed during clinical studies. We joined nursing students from other colleges and schools to begin rotations through two three-month affiliations with specialty hospitals: one pediatric and the other a state psychiatric facility.

Our class had dwindled from the "freshman forty-five" girls to twenty-seven young women by the next September as we began our third year of instruction. We received the much-coveted, blue velvet "senior" stripes to affix across our caps.

I had very little spending money. Mom sent a dollar or two when she could, and I spent it on drugstore items. Although we had a school physician, a dentist was still out of the question. I sucked on aspirins to stop the pain from cavities in my back teeth. My ears rang constantly.

While on affiliation late that fall, I met a handsome young hospital orderly. Although younger than I, "John" was a great dancer and the life of many gatherings. He spun exciting tales from his past. Even though we saw each other every weekend, we seldom spent time alone, frequenting a club popular with student nurses and hospital staff. Neither of us owned a vehicle, but we could walk to our hangout and it didn't have a cover charge. We danced all evening and made each watery beer last until it was time to run back to the dorm to make curfew.

Several classmates sported new engagement rings they'd received at Christmas. At a formal winter dance, John, wafting his usual English Leather cologne, grinned and pulled me close for a slow dance. Muscles bulged beneath his new shirt, and I snuggled against the lapel of his sport coat. I felt rapid heartbeats beneath my palm on his chest. As soon as we joined the others at our table, he surprised me with a pear-shaped diamond ring and a proposal. Happy, carefree, and blushing, I accepted. My classmates applauded.

The physical side of our relationship escalated. John worked constantly at breaking my resolve to remain "good." Using tactics I suppose that are as old as man, he often pointed out that he needed me. "And besides, in less than a year we'll be married, so what difference does it make?" Finally, during one steamy make-out session I agreed I loved him enough to take the next step. I stipulated, however, that I wouldn't feel right unless we were in a real bed, not in someone's car. I'm not sure where he borrowed the money, but on our next date we walked downtown to a small inn. The setting came straight out of a movie cast in Vermont: a canopied four-poster bed, maple country furniture, and ruffled chintz everywhere. Romantic, lovely, but...

He was more than ready. Frantic would be more accurate.

I couldn't go through with it.

I cried.

Red-faced and steaming mad, John checked us out less than thirty minutes after our arrival. The smirking desk clerk added to both my embarrassment and his anger. Leaving me trailing behind, John hissed over his shoulder as he stormed ahead. "I thought you loved me."

I pushed through the lobby doors to follow him out to the street. "I'm sorry, baby. I thought I could, but..."

"Forget it! I just hope you know you ruined our weekend."

We walked backed to the hospital, John striding fast, me in tears, scurrying along to keep up. He stopped in front of my dorm long enough to spit out, "I'll see you later." His eyes bore into mine until I looked down at the sidewalk. He leaned close, and I felt his hot breath as he snarled into my ear. "Maybe."

It took a few days for him to calm down—and for me to quit apologizing. A week later, in hopes of gaining a fresh start, I arranged to borrow a car for us to drive to Glens Falls so John could meet my family. Our relationship became smooth once again, and I relaxed and rested my head on John's shoulder while he drove. As a future bride, I looked forward to showing off my man, my ring, and in general getting some attention.

Warm enough weather meant we could lounge around on the terrace. We had a beautiful time of much laughter and teasing from my brothers. I announced we'd be married in about a year but had yet to set a date. Dave, temporarily living at Mom's with his wife and young son, quickly commented on his relief that obviously there wasn't to be a "shotgun wedding." I blushed furiously as John announced, "That's for sure!"

When Dale and his family arrived, the teasing continued, most often about my frosted hair making me a "dizzy blonde." Rather than the streaks of pale Marilyn Monroe blonde I'd asked for, the stripped and colored strands had turned out a tad pink against my dark hair. I still thought I looked sophisticated. Mom joined in and managed to mortify me at dinner, quipping, "By the way, what did you do to your hair? You look like a skunk."

On Sunday afternoon, Mom walked me to the far side of the terrace. "There's something not right here, you know. You haven't met John's family or even spoken with them by telephone, have you? He's polite, and I like that, but he seems so young, Donna." Typical of my mother, she got right to the point. "He's an orderly! Without an education or any skills, I'm worried about his earning potential." She reached up to brush the "skunk" hair away from my forehead.

I flinched at her touch and stepped back.

She pulled her hand away, sighed, looked past me toward a large planter of scarlet geraniums for a minute, and then stood a little taller. She wasn't finished. "I think you need to know John better before you make any commitments, Donna. He can't even afford an apartment or a car for himself." Then she delivered one of her famous zingers. "Are you two planning to live in the men's dorm?"

How dare she question my choices! I was quite capable of running my own life. I came up with what I hoped would be a stinging response. "You worry too much, Mom."

My mother's fears seemed unrealistic, and yet, something in the back of my mind niggled at me. I knew John and I had two things in common. We were young and poor. Certain of my future and determined to prove it, marriage seemed the next step. I knew everything would sort itself out later.

Winter flew by. I posed for my senior portrait and tailored graduation uniform fittings. I had exams to take, yearbook photography responsibilities, and a hundred other details to address before graduation in September.

The future seemed chock-full of promise. I'd graduate soon. I'd make enough money to buy a great house somewhere. I put on love's blinders and joined other engaged classmates in the pursuit of an evasive happily ever after.

CHAPTER EIGHT

One late afternoon as John retrieved a sweater from his closet, I noticed a pair of skis with a price sticker on the bottom. Wondering when he'd purchased such a luxury, I asked, "When did you buy these new skis?"

"They're not new," he called from inside the closet. "They're my lucky skis. I've won four downhill races in those."

Thinking he must have another pair somewhere in the room, I persisted. "No, *these* skis, here in the corner."

John flew out of the closet, shouting at me, "I told you those were my lucky skis. I use them all the time."

There were two other couples in the room with us, and John's response embarrassed me too much to say anything more. His refusal to admit that this pair of skis was new also angered me. I stayed silent as our friends shot questioning looks at me and appeared uncomfortable at witnessing my embarrassment.

As is my way, I waited an hour or so after we arrived at the dance hall before I attempted to make any further sense of it. While we danced a slow fox trot, I weighed my words carefully. "Honey, you obviously didn't see when I pointed to the *new* skis this afternoon."

A look of fury swept across John's face. He turned and walked off the dance floor.

Days later, John remained adamant that those same skis had carried him through two seasons of winning races. Incredibly, somehow in his mind, no ice, rocks, or frequent use would be enough to wear the price stickers off their pristine finish.

As his stories continued, people laughed at their unpredictable and incredible wildness. I began to doubt much of their content. No matter how I broached a clarification, it ended in one of three ways: he pouted in silence, walked away, or ranted at me until I cried. Embarrassment overcame happiness, and rather than excusing him, I found myself shrugging to my friends as he made illogical statements. Gobbling second helpings in misery, I gained a few pounds and pulled away physically and emotionally in confused silence.

• • •

When affiliation studies ended, I returned to Albany. The days flew by with few opportunities for John and me to see one another. When he could borrow a car, he pressured me even harder for sex; I sweated and petted but wouldn't give in. I relished the sense of power I felt over myself as much as over someone much bigger and stronger. I also felt flattered that he wanted me, and even though he moaned and groaned, I loved him even more when he appeased my demands that we'd gone far enough. Other times I came back to the dorm miffed and frustrated—couldn't we ever just have a nice time together?

The fresh bloom of romance faded during our long-distance conversations. Perhaps it was because John lived seventy miles away, or it was possible that the niggling came more often as John's stories spun even further out of control and he truly didn't seem able to tell fact from fiction. My classmates no longer found him amusing; in fact, more than one called him a liar. I wouldn't admit that the label fit as a symptom of mental disease. Instead, I chose to joke about his "little white lies" in an attempt to mask my turmoil.

I felt trapped. I wanted to get married. I'd given my word when I accepted John's proposal. How could I back out now? I stayed busy at school, and although he begged to see me, I declined to go home when I had time off. I knew that John had no place to stay in Albany, so visiting me at school wasn't an affordable option.

Knowing deep inside that I couldn't make things right, yet not wanting a confrontation, I avoided John every way I could, even his phone calls. I asked classmates to say I wasn't in the dorm. Meanwhile, I worried constantly about the effect of my maneuvers on John. After more than a month of ducking his calls and fearful about his mental state, I answered one of his calls. In an instant I heard the desperation in his voice.

"I haven't seen you in weeks!" He sounded close to tears. "I never imagined our engagement would go like this. I miss you so much, Donna."

Closing my eyes didn't block the visions I had of his face. He was right—I didn't imagine our engagement would go this way either. I felt small and mean. "I'm sorry, John. I've just been so busy…"

"Pulleez tell me you're off this weekend."

Hearing that aching hope in his voice, I couldn't lie another minute. After all, wasn't that what I accused him of?

"Yes," I whispered. "I'm going home Friday. You can come up if you can borrow a car."

"I'll be there."

I called Mom collect, hoping she'd be home over the weekend. I needed her advice, even if it meant admitting she might've been right all along.

"No, honey, I'll be leaving tomorrow for a three-week job on Long Island. Maybe you can come home when I get back."

"Mom?" *Where should I start?*

"Sweetie, did you need something?"

"No, uh, I just wanted to ask if it's okay if John comes up this weekend."

"Sure. I'll put fresh sheets on the daybed in the den. You two going out someplace special?"

"No, he and I have a few things to talk about, and I don't think they should wait." I didn't really want to get into it right then— long-distance calls in the sixties were far too expensive.

"Well, I'm disappointed I'll miss you." She paused a minute. "Is everything okay?"

She knew me too well. I eluded further discussion with, "Sure, I'm fine—just studying for exams. I'll see you sometime after you get back. Gotta go, Mom. Love you."

Bits of John's stories haunted me. He claimed so many things—winning races, rescuing strangers from a mudslide, losing a twin sister—but the details always seemed implausible. I felt that perhaps his mom or dad might shed some light on his personality. I asked about when I might meet his family—at least by telephone—but the call never took place.

How could I trust John to tell me the truth about anything? How would it be always to doubt your own husband? I knew the path I must choose, but when I thought about ending my engagement, I wept for both of us. Pain gnawed my gut as though I'd eaten glass potato chips.

Chapter Nine

Chewing the inside of my lip, I gazed out the bus window and planned my speech. Late afternoon sun clung to the landscape like outstretched fingers. Farms along Route 87 North flashed new crops of green and golden yellow. Fawn and white Guernsey cows plodded single file through a pasture gate where a black dog ushered them toward a red barn. The days had begun to lengthen by now, but a few lights shone from house windows by the time our driver pulled in to the station and parked.

I crossed South Street and stopped at a liquor store before I headed toward home. Behind a counter at the back of the store, an older man looked up from his perch and raised a tufted white eyebrow. While I studied the rows and rows of bottles, he snapped open a telltale brown bag.

Nervous but determined to keep this light, I tipped my hand of inexperience. "I've never had this one before." I placed the Johnny Walker Black Label on the counter and unzipped my clutch. "How do you mix it?"

"Well, most people drink it over ice with a little water." His rheumy eyes probed.

"Hmmm. Guess it tastes okay, huh?"

He shrugged and poked a misshapen arthritic finger at the register keys.

I counted out seven precious one-dollar bills.

Shaking his head, he handed me my change and turned back to his newspaper.

I wrapped the bag inside my sweater and hurried out the door.

Preparing to give myself the courage to end my engagement, I placed the scotch on the kitchen counter. Mom's open shelves held a variety of elegant glassware; however, I felt anything but elegant. I half-filled a Flintstones jelly glass. While no stranger to beer, I'd never been able to afford drinking the hard stuff.

The first swallow of Johnnie Walker Black Label sucked the breath out of me like Mom's Electrolux.

Adding water didn't help its taste. The squeaking of the aluminum ice tray grated my nerves raw until my tugging at the handle released several cubes. Despite chilling the amber liquid, each sip burned like fire. Holding my breath, I downed the remainder of the bitter gall with a spasmodic shudder. My hands shook as I poured another portion for good measure.

Careful to use a coaster, I placed the jelly glass filled with fresh ice and about an inch of scotch on Mom's good Sheraton table. My head spun as I sank into her favorite chair. *I wish she were here now; she'd know how to do this.* It took a few tries, but I managed to untie my sneakers and kick them off. One sailed over by the fireplace, landing in a spotlight of afternoon sun from the window. The other landed on the couch. No matter—it looked fine over there.

By now, I felt very relaxed. I closed my eyes and let my head drift toward the back of the chair. Heavy, it kept tilting until I thought it might roll off onto the floor. My brain spun like a pinwheel, yet somehow everything seemed clearer. I rehearsed. *I don't need a scene. Our relationship is over.* I imagined me saying, "Let's go our separate ways," and him, complacent and agreeable.

I awoke to the sound of loud knocking at the front door.

The living room was dark, and I switched on a lamp beside me. I cleared my throat and called out, "Come on in."

He answered from the hall, "Anyone I love in here?"

Ice clinked as I swigged the last of the scotch. Cold liquid scalded the back of my throat.

Smiling, John walked in to the living room. Despite a new plaid shirt and pressed chinos, dark circles under his eyes and unshaven face exposed the rawness of his past few weeks.

Gripping the arms of the chair, I blurted, "I can't marry you!"

His face paled as his whole body sagged. "Wwhaat…"

I knew I had a plan, an easy way to say this, but for the life of me, I couldn't recall how it went. I rolled on in a relentless, slurred ramble. "I don't want to argue about this."

He looked so bewildered, I had to get out of there.

"I'm sorry—I know you drove a long way to see me." I pushed myself up, swayed like a pine in a storm, and staggered toward the dining room. Catching the doorframe, I looked back at John and attempted a smile. "You can sleep in the den tonight, but you'll have to leave in the morning. I'm going up to bed."

His mouth stood open, his eyes locked on me.

My words came out in a croak as a finger of guilt jabbed at my throat. "The daybed's all made up and ready for you."

He blinked several times.

"Uh, I'll make you a nice breakfast before you go."

John never uttered a word, but the loudness of his silence hurt my ears.

Bent low and forward, I used the banister to pull myself up the stairs. Bracing against the wall outside the bathroom, I passed down the hallway, took three steps into my room, and collapsed, clothes and all, across my twin bed. My eyes closed as the room spun and tilted.

I dreamed something rough and hard scraped at my mouth, pressing my head deep into the pillow. Dizzy, groggy, I writhed against its pressure. What was happening?

I couldn't wake up. Light from the bathroom down the hallway made little impact. I suddenly recognized an overwhelming scent of English Leather and the strong impatient hand probing under my shirt.

I tried to brush it away. "Hey, wait a minute—I don't ..." Numb and uncoordinated from the liquor, I had no strength.

His knee painfully crushed my thigh into the mattress as his hand jerked down to my jeans. My right arm pinned, I struggled harder to push him away with my left. "Stop! Get off me, John. What are you doing?"

Silent, his movements came faster. Rougher.

I fought and scratched, screamed all the profanities I'd ever heard.

Below the grunting, the bed creaked and pitched until he finished. He pushed himself off me and stood beside the bed, his breathing rapid and loud.

Stunned, childlike and submissive, I lay still as he pulled up his shorts and pants. He loomed close over me again.

Cringing, I tugged my shirt down over my breasts and reached down to cover my groin.

He caught my left hand and held it tight as he yanked the engagement ring off my finger.

Tears blurred the sight of John walking down the hall toward the light. I heard him clunk down the stairs. The nauseating combination of sweat and semen overpowered the aftershave scent on my shoulder.

Gagging, trying to be quiet, I slid off the bed and let my jeans and panties fall to the floor. My thighs felt both slick and sticky. Terrified he might still be in the house, I strained to hear any telltale footsteps or movement. When I heard the front door slam downstairs, I crept to the bathroom.

I covered my face and stood in the corner of the shower letting hot water cascade over my shoulders, down my back. I would never feel clean again. Or young. Or carefree.

The person I once believed I'd marry disappeared from my life that night. Our engagement lasted four months. I made weak excuses to my family about not being the right time to get married and blamed the termination on myself. I didn't report the rape. I didn't tell anyone about drinking myself into a stupor or that I'd been powerless to prevent what happened next. I didn't talk to Dad or my brothers about the details of that night. I never even told my mother.

For the next three and a half decades, I pushed away the sad, sudden, and violent conclusion of that promise-filled future and the life I thought I'd wanted. It took a long time for me to forgive John—and myself—but I have.

Only in the recent past has society and, indeed, law enforcement recognized that girls didn't "ask for it," that they meant it when they said "no," or that rape victims suffered a most horrific violation of their person.

Chapter Ten

I studied my calendar in a vain attempt to reschedule the past. Enough days had passed since the last red Xs marking my period that I worried I might start when I was unprepared—at the hospital, in the middle of a class, or during a mixed doubles game of tennis. At twenty, I was naïve—even for the gloved-and-girdled sixties. Before I slept each night, I prayed to the God I sought in times of trouble. "Please, God, let my period start tonight."

Two weeks passed. More prayers filled with bargaining promises of regular church attendance, careful guarding of my language, I even dusted off my father's Masonic Bible.

During the day, if I experienced a cramp or stomach rumbling, hope shot up like an untamed plant. I refused to believe anything could be wrong. Other than feeling a little tired, as long as I followed the routines of nursing and studies, everything seemed normal.

I began to avoid my close friends, fearing I might break down enough to reveal my concerns. After a while, they stopped coming by my room when I didn't invite them inside. Exhausted but sleepless with worry, I stayed up late, spending several hours in the dorm kitchen each night. As classmates came and went after taking breaks from finals' studies or after working the evening shift, I lingered. I joined in each of their animated discussions of where they wanted to live after graduation, what type of nursing they'd do, and which hospitals paid the best. I did everything I could imagine to remain excited and hopeful about my future.

By midnight, the dorm was dark and quiet. Facing fear meant returning to my room when I could no longer keep myself awake. My room had always been a popular room, which in happier times held music and noisy students whose laughter spilled into the hallways. As I readied for bed, I studied myself in the mirror over the sink. My face looked like it always did; my eyes were the same blue. I turned sideways. Although my stomach felt full, my waist remained small. Somehow, my breasts seemed larger, my nipples darkened. I covered them with a nightie and slipped beneath the sheets. My hopes for something different spun away into the forlorn night. Although I refused even to utter the word *pregnant* to myself in the dark, I stopped praying one of those forlorn nights.

• • •

I picked a physician's name from the Yellow Pages and set up an appointment. I wished I could ask a friend to go along, but I couldn't. I used a made-up name when I registered at the doctor's office to confirm my fearful suspicion. I tried my best to look calm and nonchalant as I settled in a corner chair and thumbed through an old, tattered magazine. Although there were several other women seated in the room, no one spoke; they looked at magazines too.

Eons later a tall, unsmiling nurse appeared at the doorway leading past the reception area. She consulted the manila folder in her hand and snapped off a name in a loud, raspy voice.

No one moved.

Peering over her half glasses, she surveyed me and the other three women in the room.

We patients looked at one another, gave tiny apologetic smiles and shrugs, and went back to our magazines.

Imperious, the nurse rasped the name two more times before I realized she summoned me using my made-up name.

My head shot up, and my eyes found hers staring at me. I gasped a faint, "Oh, that's me." I wanted to be invisible. I grabbed for my red corduroy purse, fumbled, and dropped it on the floor. I felt my face grow hot and knew it blazed bright sunburn pink. My hand shook as I placed the magazine I'd pretended to read onto the table beside me. My legs turned to rubber when I rose. I wasn't sure they could hold me. I kept my head down, but as I moved past the woman nearest me, I noticed her open stare and thought I heard a sharp *tsk* sound.

In silent misery, I followed the nurse until she stopped in a small alcove with a wall-hung desk and a scale. "Open," she commanded as she shook down a thermometer and pointed to the scale. Her breath smelled of onions.

I stepped onto the platform, felt it jiggle beneath me, and heard the weighted arm rattle. I opened my mouth but couldn't help jerking back as she jabbed the thermometer into the base of my tongue. I tried to bite the glass enough to steady the thermometer, but it continued to tremble while she weighed me and wrote in my chart.

"Now, go in the bathroom across the hall and get me a urine sample."

I urinated often these days but had trouble getting even a dribble into the specimen cup. I wrapped the cup in a paper towel, washed my hands, and tried to smile as I emerged from the bathroom. "Here you go," I said in my cheeriest, let's-at-least-be-friendly voice as I set the container on the counter.

The nurse responded with a bare nod and then said, "Sit on that stool."

I cringed at the difference between her attitudes toward me compared to my trained response to patients. I abandoned my resolve to be open to her and dubbed her Nurse Wretched.

Bending over my chart, she never looked at me as she fired off questions about my family's health history.

She had me so unnerved I could only whisper my answers.

It came at me like a sledgehammer. "When was your last period?"

My face burned as I squirmed on the seat, trying to remember. "I'm not certain. I think...sometime in the middle of April?" It came out as a question—like she should know the answer.

"Have you experienced any nausea?"

"No, I feel fine."

"Are your breasts tender?"

Before I could answer, my arm rose until my splayed fingers pressed my breast as though directed by someone else. "No."

Nurse Wretched bent farther over the desk, scribbling. The pearl chain dangling from her glasses' frame dragged across the desk, catching and scattering a stack of lab slips. "Are you regular?"

I smiled at this one. "Oh, yes. Very regular—I go every day."

She stopped straightening the lab slips and glared at me. Deep creases made her eyebrows almost meet in the middle as she frowned. "Oh, for heaven's sake, are your *periods* regular?"

Tears started down my cheeks. I licked one away from the corner of my mouth, lowered my head, and nodded yes. I couldn't find another word.

· · ·

Without even the smallest attempt at warmth or friendliness, the nurse led me down a dark hallway, opened a door, stepped aside, and waited for me to enter. As I passed her, she handed me a folded sheet and said, "Make sure your bladder's empty. When you're ready, sit on the end of the table and put this on your lap."

I tried to appear blasé. Too nervous to recall what I might have learned from the day I spent in the gynecologist's office a year earlier, I didn't ask what "ready" implied. I entered the small room, colliding with the end of an old wooden exam table. A tall gooseneck lamp sat beside the table, a brown metal folding chair in the corner.

Uncertain about what to do next, I left my clothing and shoes on and wrapped the sheet around my waist. The table creaked as I stepped onto its square platform. Shivering, I sat and waited, counting dirty spots on the floor beyond my swinging feet.

The Yellow Pages physician turned out to be fat, old, and brusque. Coming through the door, he slammed my chart onto the countertop, tugged on a pair of gloves, and turned toward me.

I smiled and tried to ignore the yellowed wet stains beneath his armpits.

Without introduction or greeting, he ensconced himself on a rolling stool. Scooting close to the foot of the table, he glared up at me, apparently expecting me to position myself.

I sat there, unmoving, scared stiff.

His large face turned purple. "Well, put your feet in the stirrups and slide on down here!"

Had I not been scared witless, the fact I still had my panties on under my dress as I placed my feet in the stirrups might have been funny. Nurse Wretched stood next to me but didn't reach to hold my hand, assist me, or even touch my shoulder; she did nothing. *This woman cannot be a real nurse.*

Out of my sight, the doctor shouted, "You're making it *impossible* to work. Get your underwear off." He sat back, arms folded across his big belly, and leered while I slid off the table, tearing the paper covering as I went. I turned my back to peel down my underpants. Sweat trickled down my bared backside.

My face felt hot enough that I realized it was beet red, but somehow I managed to place my underwear on the corner chair. Seeing the paper on the table dampened from my sweat mortified me. I forced myself to climb back onto the creaking table and positioned myself on the edge for my first pelvic examination. I gripped the sides of the table beneath me and strained to lift my legs into the stirrups without falling off the end.

Idle, Nurse Wretched stood by, arms folded, waiting and watching.

The appointment culminated with even more embarrassment as the doctor finished his brief, rough examination. His voice boomed loud enough to hear across Albany, "You're pregnant."

I heard his words. They didn't register, but his next ones did. Before I could even pull myself upright, the visit turned from unbearable to horrid when he slapped my quivering thigh.

"So, do ya wanna get rid of it?"

Appalled to my very soul, I jerked upright. My eyes stung. Random, racing thoughts collided. I knew only that I had to escape this place. This man and his wretched nurse. This moment.

Yanking my madras shirtwaist dress down, I slid off the table and pushed past him. I ran through the hallway, threw a five- and a ten-dollar bill in the general direction of the receptionist, and fled out the door.

My panties may still be on the chair.

Chapter Eleven

The very thought of being pregnant scared me stiff. Being alone made me feel angry, and I felt grown-up and childlike all at the same time. I wanted to run away from school and the future. I felt incredibly sickened with embarrassment.

I needed my mother. I wanted my father.

Like a kid watching the night sky for Santa Claus, I clung to the hope of a miracle—a phenomenon like that awful doctor making a mistake in my exam, or a fairy-tale Prince Charming swooping me away to a blissful marriage—anything but being pregnant. In miserable silence, I waited for the miracle.

I remained pregnant.

While visiting Dad a week later, I stood at the top of his steep stairs. It flashed through my mind to purposely miss a step and plunge to the bottom. In the movies, such a fall always caused a miscarriage. My heart knew I couldn't take that way out. White-knuckled, I clung tight to the banister and descended the stairway.

Every night I drifted off to sleep with the same thought swirling around me—I could never harm a baby. Every morning that resolve grew with the child inside me. Numb for days, like a woman with an anesthetized soul, I plodded through shift work and studies.

In the downstairs lounge area one evening after dinner, incessant dorm talk of work opportunities for graduates bombarded me. I posed classmates for their yearbook photographs and focused the camera on groups of committee members arranging themselves on chairs and couches. I mimicked their excited chatter about our futures, although I had yet to come to grips with mine. My world encompassed a huge blur of unending uncertainty.

Up until that point, I'd had no morning sickness, only a faint sense of fatigue. I felt normal and ordinary, gliding underwater in a warm, tropic sea—until the Yellow Page doctor's words crashed over me like crazy wild surf, "You're pregnant." It felt surreal. One minute I swam in calm waters below all turbulence, the next I couldn't stop myself from rising to the roaring, silver surface above me. *I am going to have a baby.* I wanted to stop swimming and rest, but the undertow kept tumbling me closer to the cold rocky bottom. Huge tender bits of my world shredded each time I slammed into the coral reefs.

Under the circumstances, I'd never seek my baby's father. My mind spilled over in a hundred different directions, but there was no escaping the reality of my situation. Cultural pressures precluded me disclosing my pregnancy to a classmate, much less the terror I endured. I showered in the wee hours of the mornings to avoid anyone seeing my nakedness. My once-small waist thickened as my nipples darkened and blue veins spread across my breasts.

Regardless of the conception circumstances, unmarried pregnant girls were objects of derisive gossip and caused their families huge embarrassment. No one could have thought worse of me than I did.

I longed to rush into my father's strong arms. He and Marianne had several young children by now, and although no longer his little girl, I still sought his approval. I ached to hear him tell me to be brave one more time—that everything would be okay. My brothers were both married and had babies of their own.

Most of all, I ached for the peace of my mother's pink bedroom, slipping into her bed and hearing her say she'd help me hold my head up—that we'd make it. Mom still struggled with her own finances, working harder than ever as a nanny. In fact, she'd just finished two jobs on Long Island—working for sixteen dollars a day. Her strength in tough times had taught me your world can crash, but you alone decide whether it burns. Although I felt she was my best friend and I longed to talk to her, consuming shame silenced me.

I resolved not to tell my family of my predicament. I stopped visits home. I couldn't bear to allow them to see my growing dishonor.

Besides my eliminated family, I couldn't think of anyone in whom I could confide. I didn't understand another woman's empathy or the heart's capacity to love. Anticipating everyone's rejection, I didn't tell a soul.

I'd been brave before.

• • •

Both the hours of practice and crossing the bay on my own turned me into a confident swimmer. In the midst of my father's annual choir picnic, dozens of eyes focused on twenty unconditioned adults spreading out, attempting Dad's "swim across the bay challenge." Several boats accompanied the swimmers. More than a few shivering stragglers, pulled to safety, sprawled across the seats like beached whales.

Playing on shore, I heard a commotion and screams of "Somebody get her!" Half a dozen hands pointed to a girl flailing in the deep water far past the end of the dock. None of her peers seemed to be helping; everyone else stood up on the new sundeck roof or swam, far away. I raced along the dock, pushing hysterical girls aside. I belly flopped off the diving board and kicked as hard as I could. Making the worst possible move, I swam straight toward the girl who I could now recognized as Carol, a twelve-year-old from Dad's junior choir.

In total panic, she grabbed me, shoved me underwater, and climbed my body like a ladder. Carol's nails and bony knees dug into me, and I struggled but couldn't escape her death grip. Exhausted from both my race to get to her and fighting for advantage, I tried to gain way to the top. She pushed me down twice before I could take even one breath.

I heard the distorted underwater sounds of Carol's coughing, gasping gulps of the air I so desperately needed. From beneath her, I saw the lake's mirrored undersurface far above my head. I felt cold through my entire body, even though I could see a remote shimmering sun.

Sheer survival instinct took over. Unable to extend my arms while she pinned them, I stretched my hand up along her back. As Carol's head tipped back to keep her face out of the water, I twisted a handful of her long hair into my fingers and pulled for dear life, swimming upwards. Stunned by my painful yanking, she released me, but I hung on to her hair and towed her toward the dock.

Hearing the hullabaloo below, my mother traversed the length of the sundeck, clamored down the stairs, ran out to the dock's end, and climbed down the ladder.

Focused on Mom's familiar arm stretching toward me, I tugged harder at my heavy load. I struggled forward, not considering I still could drown from exhaustion or from Carol breaking free and commencing the fight for her life—after all, I was just six years old. I only knew I had to help a girl in trouble. I swam and fought with every fiber of my being to save her.

Momma leaned far out to catch an arm.

Carol was fine.

Someone lifted me out of the water. I sagged against a post, slid down onto my bottom, and felt glorious, warm sunshine on my face.

• • •

The summer passed, yearbooks were distributed, and that fall I joined countless other nursing seniors across the nation in the ritual of signing fond notes to fellow graduates. For the past three years, I'd longed for independence to start my career, yet now I found myself fearful of the future. Dread of leaving this safe cocoon tainted my happiness and sense of pride at finishing nursing school.

Quick, darting butterflies low in my abdomen reminded me I didn't face the next step alone. This miniature being's feather-light kicks reinforced the fact of its total dependence upon me.

I asked myself a thousand questions. What am I going to do? Where should I go? Where could I work? What happens if I can't get a job because I'm pregnant? Being unemployable was a very real possibility. My situation seemed immense, almost impossible. Going back to Glens Falls was out of the question. A collective, rigid bigotry toward having a child out of wedlock demanded women like me move out of town. I could not and would not shame my parents.

I stumbled toward an uncertain future as I settled on a plan to move two hundred miles away from my family.

On a conscious level, I prayed at the beginning of my pregnancy to make it disappear, somehow to be a mistake. And now with my life so out of balance, I didn't think to ask for God's help. My courage staggered against its weight.

In a dark gray blur, I sent out graduation invitations, completed final courses, and packed my belongings. Fortunate to be tall, I didn't "show" when I graduated, although buttoning my starched-stiff uniform took some time. Appearing in front of a crowd made me nervous, and from the last glance in the mirror, I knew my blushing cheeks matched the pink roses I carried.

They called our names in alphabetical order. I edged to the front of my chair, heard my name, and prayed my legs wouldn't buckle as I stood. Sucking in my belly, I held my head high, looked straight ahead, and walked across the stage. I clasped our director's hand and reached for the piece of paper that would change my life.

Receiving that diploma *did* change my life. However, the moment that would alter my life forever—the moment that would cause me to know life would go on all around me while mine jerked from its predicted path—had occurred twenty weeks earlier. It was the end of September 1965, and I was halfway through my pregnancy.

CHAPTER TWELVE

Three days after graduation, two classmates and I moved across New York state from Albany to Buffalo. All our prerequisite to independent-living possessions were stuffed into two 1965 Mustang Fastbacks. Along the way when we stopped for a meal, I told them of my plight.

They looked at each other, turned to me, and assured me getting a job, finding a place to live, even having a baby would turn out okay. Each in our own thoughts, we returned to our cars. After that kind of revelation, I tried not to imagine the conversation in the other Mustang. How I wanted to make them understand, *I am still me.*

It turned out getting a job was the easiest of our tasks. Apartment hunting in Buffalo stretched into a tough search to find something habitable and affordable, even with our combined anticipated earnings. We found ourselves living out of our cars for a couple of days and eating low-cost meals. We cleaned up on occasion in a gas station restroom. In the end, we combined our graduation money and rented a furnished apartment in the former ballroom of a venerable old hotel on Delaware Avenue near downtown.

The apartment was a large room with twelve-foot tall ceilings and a marble floor. A lumpy couch, side table and lamp, and a stuffed chair with a matching ottoman perched on the worn living room rug. A chest-high bamboo divider stretched through the room, walling off a bedroom area with three twin beds. On the far side of the living area, there was a tiny butler's pantry-turned galley kitchen and a small bathroom with a sink and claw foot tub.

While my roommates worked in surgery at Buffalo Children's Hospital, I chose the Newborn Nursery at Buffalo General Hospital. I rationalized, *I can find the best obstetrician there—after I know how he is with his patients.* I chose a young fellow with twinkling blue eyes, a crew cut, and a ready smile. Dr. Maurice Dewey had great rapport with the maternity floor nurses, who endorsed my choice and told me his patients adored him.

. . .

Like many Yankees, I loved the sharp morning air of fall. I leaned on the driver's door as the pump chugged fuel into the gas tank. It took five dollars to fill it up. The attendant was busy with another car, so I counted out five ones and walked into the toasty warm station to pay. Outside again, hints of winter gusted swirling russet leaves around my feet. I pulled my sweater tight around my growing belly. It was my day off. At eleven o'clock in the morning, I would meet the obstetrician my coworkers recommended.

My first tearful visit confirmed Dr. Maurice Dewey's compassionate nature. Over the next two visits, as I confessed my fears and expectations of the future with a baby, he guided me toward a practical course. He didn't push me in any direction but opened my eyes to what life with a child and no spouse might be like.

"Donna, if your final decision is to give up your baby, I'll do my best to find the right family. I have a long list of couples who can't have their own and want to adopt."

I wrestled constantly with looming decisions, bowed by the weight of the practical daily aspects of single parenthood. I'd only begun working in October. As a graduate nurse, I didn't make enough to have any savings. If I passed my state nursing board examinations, I'd become a licensed registered nurse and increase my earnings somewhat.

To celebrate my graduation, my sweet mother had scrimped and saved enough money to make a down payment on a brand new

Mustang. Dale selected the trendy car, and I loved its dark turquoise paint, white interior, and flashy silhouette. Neither my mother nor my brother was aware of my pending financial strain. Much as I loved my new "Bluebird," I faced car payments of seventy-eight dollars a month.

Since our rent agreement didn't allow tenants with children, keeping my baby would necessitate my moving to furnished, affordable housing with laundry facilities. Big-city living taught me a suitable apartment must also be safe. As cold air seeped inside from around every one of our windows, the necessity of a place that could be kept warm during Buffalo's well-known freezing winters became an important factor.

It'd been very difficult for my roommates and me to find a place with even the minimal standards. We'd achieved the affordable and laundry facilities parts. Furnished, one-bedroom apartment rents averaged around $120 per month then, and even with three salaries, we didn't always eat well. I grossed about $370 a month. That didn't leave much for utilities, food, car expenses, insurance, or emergencies.

I didn't dare ask my roommates if they wanted to live with a new baby and me. I felt sure I knew the answer. Even if I found used baby furniture, I would need a number of new items. The list seemed endless: diapers, bottles, sterilizer, formula, clothing, stroller… Given the circumstances, I couldn't expect any baby shower.

Worst of all, my heart carried the weight of a thousand boulders as I speculated about who would watch my baby while I worked to support us. At the time, facilities offering to care for children under the age of three were rare, seldom licensed, and paid their employees meager wages. Like charitable endeavors for the very poor, they reminded me of the hapless orphanages of Charles Dickens's writings.

I had firsthand knowledge of the aides who worked for low wages in the hospital nursery. Most seemed to be all business and seldom cuddled our tiny infants. Many of them were moms, but they wouldn't allow wailing babies to interrupt their work routines. We stayed on our feet almost all shift, hustling babies back and forth to their mothers' rooms, changing diapers every few hours, cleaning up newborns, feeding preemies every two hours. The hospital nursery saw frequent staff turnovers.

It took little imagination to envision what kind of attention similar workers might dole out to working mothers' children. I shuddered at the prospect of my baby in such a place, gaining independence, toddling about, demonstrating the terrible twos. The thought of placing my own baby in the hands of a series of strangers throughout his childhood brought on weeks of new sweat-drenched nightmares.

How will I manage if the baby gets sick? I conjured up images of the very sick children I'd cared for in the pediatric hospital as a student. *What happens to us if I get sick?*

Try as I might, without family assistance—which I felt was out of the question—I couldn't fathom how I could care for an infant, much less raise a child by myself. The possibility of Dr. Dewey finding the "right family" for the infant I'd deliver became my sole comfort.

• • •

While the cold months of a stormy winter near Lake Erie dragged by, the increasing movement of what I envisioned as my own little athlete warmed me. As charge nurse of the evening shift, I got home from work near midnight and often shoveled my way into our apartment's parking lot.

Exhausted, I sank into an armchair, propped up my swollen feet on the ottoman, and snatched a few moments of quiet over a cup of cocoa before retiring. As soon as I sat down, inevitable antics commenced. Still certain I carried a little boy, I envisioned baby aquatic stretches, tumbling, and dozens of flip-turns at the ends of his private pool. I discovered when I sang hymns, lullabies, or Christmas carols in a soft voice, my little Olympian would become still and quiet.

I shooed the neighbor's tomcat out the window and collapsed into my single bed for a night's rest. My roommates slept in their beds beside me in the dark. It was such a lonesome time.

Phone calls from my mother covered one topic: she couldn't understand why even a new nurse had to work Thanksgiving, Christmas, and New Year's Eve. She told me often how much she missed me. Her next question was always the same, "When are you coming home, honey?"

I crossed my fingers and lied, "Mom, I'm sure I'll have a three-day weekend scheduled soon."

Meanwhile, my roommates worked the day shift and left for work around six o'clock in the morning. They were fast asleep when I got home near midnight. If they happened to be off for a couple of days, they were often out when I came in, or had gone home for a visit. As they came and went through holiday parties, I found myself tinged with wistful envy. Except for two guys who lived next door, I didn't know the tenants in our building. They, too, went out most evenings and weren't home in the daytime.

Growing larger and more miserable each week, I'm sure I was seldom good company for my roommates. To boost my flagging spirits, I picked up a crooked, bargain-priced Scotch pine. I placed a few meager Christmas decorations on the odd little tree. The cat crowded into my disappearing lap every night. While I listened to Doris Day, Andy Williams, and Herb Albert music, I learned to knit. In quiet voices, the cat and I sang away the nights.

Dr. Dewey and I didn't discuss the cost of my delivery. As I had at the beginning of my pregnancy, I felt avoiding the issue might make it go away. Not certain how much money I'd need for my hospitalization, I lived a frugal existence. I seldom went anywhere but to work, and even a McDonald's hamburger seemed too expensive.

I wore scrub dresses at work. At home, I combined four items into maternity outfits—a red pullover, a madras plaid shirt, black wool slacks, and a gray wool skirt. My coat no longer buttoned. I warded off the apartment's chill with a shapeless gray cardigan and knee socks. I couldn't have impressed anyone with my ensembles.

In mid-December, I splurged and bought one hundred red and green pom-poms. I stapled one of each color to the tops of the tiny disposable white caps our newborns wore in the hospital. At feeding time on Christmas Eve, I brought each infant out to its mother adorned in a miniature Santa hat topped with red and green.

That night, while the babies spent time with their mothers, I fed another whose momma was running a fever and too ill to give her son a bottle. For a few minutes after he ate, I held him close to my shoulder, rocked him in a slow, gentle motion, and sang "Silent Night" to two babies. One I held in my arms, the other safe within me—for just a few more weeks. I wondered if the infant in my belly felt alone. I wondered if he knew how often I worried about his future.

I couldn't find even a tiny smile for the usual stream of jovial passersby. I turned the rocker away from the nursery windows.

I felt well and never caught so much as a cold, but by New Year's Eve, I moved slower as I passed out 7UP cocktails to our new mommies.

As the only RN on my shift, I had no peers to talk to, and although I liked the two or three aides who rotated to assist in our busy nursery, we didn't socialize. The nursery census averaged forty babies, plus a couple of tiny preemies in a separate room. With the constant turnover of admissions and discharges in our metropolitan hospital, the maternity floor nurses stayed busy with their own work. None of us had much time to chat, and few asked any questions of me—when I was due, how long I planned to work, etc. I guessed either hospital scuttlebutt or my lack of a wedding band made those questions unnecessary.

I lived in isolation from the carefree life other nurses seemed to live, but gosh, how I longed to talk to someone about stretch marks, backaches, the thumping under my ribs, and *what was labor really like, anyhow?*

I didn't realize it at the time, but a few of the postpartum nurses did know of my loneliness and circumstances and would soon share it with someone else.

• • •

In the sixties, women remained hospitalized for a week after a delivery. I brought sweet-smelling babies to their bedside for feedings. Afterward, I picked up satiated, sleepy infants to return to the nursery. During these visits, I came to know these women as they chatted about their husbands, homes, and visions for the future.

Beaming fathers were most often around on my evening shift, particularly during the holidays. As I placed tiny bundles of joy for the first time into strong, trembling arms, the moms and I laughed at the daddies' quaking.

One evening I brought a beautiful baby girl to a well-known and respected Buffalo family. I stood in the doorway and witnessed the loving bonds that gently wrapped around this little family.

How could I supply such cohesiveness, such energy, such security by myself?

As I watched them gaze with adoration at their baby, I found the answer. I loved my child enough to realize I could not. I was a mother, but I would not be a parent.

• • •

Four o'clock sun slipped across the porch boards as I climbed the stairs of the old house Dr. Dewey shared with another obstetrician as an office. Even though it'd be dark and January-cold by the time I left, I liked being here.

My checkups, scheduled at the end of the day, came more often now. Professional and patient, Dr. Dewey still joked, kidded me, and made me feel like a friend. After my exams, we talked in his office. Often though, I talked while he listened. I was anxious to talk this visit.

A little early for this appointment, I shrugged out of my coat and piled it onto my remaining lap. The clock ticked on and on as the empty waiting room chairs yawned wide. I stared through the window beside my chair. *If you decide something, that's that. But if "that's that," then why am I still feeling it's not right?* I'd tried to answer this question for days, but it still battered my weary mind.

A short, slender woman, dressed in a beautiful camel coat with a pale blue scarf came down the hallway and called out to the receptionist, "Bye—see you in six months." She dug through her purse as she walked past me. Her lipstick was the perfect shade. Her dark brown shoes matched the purse, as did the gloves she extracted from inside it. She opened the door to the porch and stepped outside. Gusts of wind buffeted her small frame, but not a hair on her head moved as she disappeared into the chilly dusk. Her earthy-sweet perfume scent lingered.

I never paid much attention to other women who visited this office. I'd slouched in a corner, intent on becoming invisible. Suddenly aware of my surroundings, the leather chairs, gilt-framed paintings, and handsome lamps that shone with understated tasteful elegance. I looked down, caring for the first time in months that my slacks had cat hairs on them, my loafers needed a polish, and my red shirt could stand some ironing.

Embarrassed, I slipped into the bathroom and captured a sample of my urine in a specimen cup. Washing my hands, I stared at my reflection in the mirror. I reached up to fluff my curls, wishing I'd brought a brush to tame some of the static electricity from my hair. Momma pushed and patted my hair in place with wet hands when I was a child. It didn't work for me now. I seldom wore makeup, but the elegant woman leaving the office made me feel ashamed of my pale face without even a smear of lipstick.

Retreating to the waiting room, I went back to my corner chair. Seventh grade insecurity revisited me, pinned me against its seat. Fighting a rising desire to run and furious at myself for looking so disheveled on this particular visit, I snatched stray cat hairs from my pant legs.

"Donna, come on back. Let's see how you're doing." The nurse held the hallway door open. Weighing me, she bantered in her usual kind way. She took my blood pressure then checked my urine specimen for sugar and protein. The clock over the scale read five thirty.

Dr. Dewey pushed the bell-shaped end of his stethoscope into several places on my abdomen. He paused, listening, and then slid the instrument to a new area. I tried to breathe as little as possible. I didn't want anything to drown out the baby's heartbeat. Another firm press of the stethoscope, and a knowing smile grew across Dr. Dewey's mouth. His face was inches from my stomach, but I heard him whisper, "There you are, you little rascal!"

He slid the shiny curved headpiece attached to the stethoscope off his head and hung it on a hook. "Baby sounds fine today." He winked at me as he stretched a measuring tape up and over the faint brown stripe on my abdomen, past my bulging belly button to an area beneath my breastbone. "Growin' well, too."

He held out his hand and helped me sit up. "Come on in my office, and we'll talk, okay?" He turned to the nurse, who held the doorknob with her hand. "Thanks for sticking around. I'll let you know when I finish surgery in the morning—should be around ten o'clock."

Dr. Dewey signed a chart on his desk as I sank into the chair in front of him. The bristles of his crew cut gleamed golden in the light from a brass desk lamp. He opened another chart on the brown leather padded area. "Hang on just a second, Donna." His scratching fountain pen made the only sound in the room. At last, he added the chart to a stack in a wooden tray marked, "Out." A much taller stack sat at his elbow. He placed the pen on the desk and smiled at me. His day seemed far from over, but he waited patiently for me to begin.

Leaning forward, I felt my throat begin to close. I didn't know how to word it—this cataclysmic decision. I swallowed the tongues of fire licking my larynx.

His expression blended confusion and patience, and above all, that's what finally made it possible to figure out the right words.

"Dr. Dewey, I…want…" My nose stung. I tried not to cry. "I can't—I need to give up my baby."

Those blue, blue eyes of his never left mine as he moved his head in a slow nod and pulled tissues from a box at the edge of the desk.

I took them as the dam behind my eyes and nose broke. "Well, what I mean is, I want you to find a home for my baby." I tried to maintain the things normal people do when they're with someone else—things like talking and breathing—but my words drowned in loud sobbing sounds rushing up through my chest in jagged shudders.

Being a physician—one who had been through all this before—he knew both my sincerity and doubts. "You're certain about this, then?"

"Yes, Dr. Dewey, I know it's best. It's a huge relief you have people waiting for a baby. But the whole thing terrifies me. I'm afraid I'll…"

Visions of a nursery with crying infants reaching over the sides of their cribs to me left me muted.

It became obvious that I wasn't able to express myself. Dr. Dewey gave a gentle prod. "Afraid about what?"

I held on to the arms of the chair to prevent me from racing for the door. "I know it's the right thing for the baby's sake, but… I mean, I'm afraid if I see the baby I won't be able to leave him."

He nodded, "I understand. You don't have to see it. Here's what we're going to do. I'll tell you if your baby is a girl or a boy, and if it's okay." In a patient, kind tone, he described how the adoption process worked. He assured me again about his list of couples seeking to adopt babies.

Rows and rows of cribs flashed through my mind, and distant wailing cries ebbed and flowed around his words.

"I'll match one of them to your looks and background. I'll make all the arrangements and have an attorney draw up the paperwork for you to sign."

As I listened, my tears gradually subsided. I hated not being able to picture someone on his list. I tried to focus on his words.

"...after you've delivered, and assuming you don't change your mind, you'll sign the papers before you leave the hospital. Do you have any more questions?"

"No, I guess not."

"Good. Everything's all set, then."

I could do nothing but sit there, watching as he wrote in my chart. Everything in my life felt out of control. I could never be happy again.

I left Dr. Dewey's office feeling as fragile as my mother's thinnest antique teacup—translucent, ready to shatter with the slightest jarring. Driving the few blocks home, the harder I clenched the steering wheel, the more I cried. I told myself I'd made the right decision.

I repeated my affirmation many times that night, and about a million more times over the next three and a half decades. Each time I confirmed the decision was right, the truth in my heart burst outside. I would never, could never forgive myself.

Chapter Thirteen

Working in a white fog of worry, I looked up to see Dr. Dewey come into the nursery. I'd waved at him passing by on his evening rounds earlier. He didn't often stop here at the end of his day. From his wedding band and photos in his office, I knew he had a family waiting somewhere.

While I changed a flailing infant, he stood nearby and watched me. I attempted to act normal, sound casual. "Can I help you, Dr. Dewey?"

"What's wrong with you tonight?"

I looked up and smiled in his direction. "Nothing."

Walking in a straight line toward me, he repeated, "What's wrong, Donna?"

"Nothing—I'm fine."

Looking exasperated, he gripped the end of the bassinette and shook his head, "Well, you're not your sunny self!"

His kind attentiveness crumbled my wall of self-defense. I blinked at the tears forming. It took a great deal of determination to not bury my face in his olive corduroy jacket and give in to the deluge I willed back.

Now in a gentle voice, he said, "Put down that baby and follow me. We need to talk a minute." He led the way into the nurses' station.

Earlier that day, while I changed into my white scrub dress in the nurse's lounge, I'd asked one of the floor nurses about available, inexpensive housing. She took the initiative to tell Dr. Dewey of my obvious distress.

Knees almost touching in the nurses' tiny office, we sat and talked. My tears flowed unabated as I told him that one roommate would soon return home to plan her wedding and long-term, the other wished to live alone. Being due to have my baby in two weeks, the stress of a potential move, having no family support, and losing the company of my only friends overwhelmed me.

He didn't hesitate for a minute.

His boyish grin crinkled his eyes as he chuckled and said, "Well, missy, you just have yourself packed by nine o'clock Saturday morning. I'm picking you up, and you're coming to our house to live."

I was astounded.

"Oh, Dr. Dewey, I can't do that! You don't even know me."

"I know you well enough."

"But, have you asked your wife?"

His face spread further into that wonderful smile I'd come to look for in the last four months. "Her name is Pam. She'll love you. I do!"

Sure enough, that Saturday Dr. Dewey moved me, my well-worn maternity clothes, sixties-modern red plastic radio, round aqua hair dryer, and lots of other "stuff" into their home. After introductions, he made it clear I should abandon my nurse's practice of formal salutation to physicians and now call him "Maurie." Pam and their two young sons welcomed me into mild chaotic domesticity.

The Deweys lived north of Buffalo in a beautiful old home across the street from Pam's parents. I had a large second-floor room to myself, next to my hosts'. I placed my clothes in the dresser and hung up my skirt and coat in the closet. Tucking my suitcase underneath, I sat on the double bed. Sunshine flooded the room, washing the wooden floors to a golden pumpkin color. Snow sparkled on the roof across the street, but I felt warm and comfortable. The bathroom stood at my end of the hallway. I washed my face and descended the creaking stairs to become acquainted with this generous couple.

Pam and Maurie were warm and solicitous, and we soon settled into work schedules, delicious meals, and heartfelt chats. Although

I still longed to see my mother, some of my loneliness dissipated in their company. I enjoyed the frequent antics of their two young sons. On the rare occasions Maurie spent an evening at home, I watched him interact with Pam. I yearned for someone like him in my life.

Pam and I grew closer each day, and I basked in the glow of her generous spirit. Her honest smile and dark eyes seemed a tonic for my own kind of personal heartburn. Pam's soft, whisper-like voice never raised—her touch, at once soft and strong. She and Maurie made me feel worthy of being loved for the first time in months.

My due date came and went.

A week later, I awoke in the night to a strange, gnawing pain low in my pelvis. It didn't last long, but instinctive understanding flooded over me as I realized I'd been feeling these pains just beneath my sleep's surface. So, this was it! The clock on the table next to me read two thirty. It was Friday, February 18.

• • •

Excited but not anxious, I forced myself to stay in bed watching the clock's luminescent hands. Fifteen minutes passed before I experienced another contraction. I felt my abdomen grow rigid as my back arched into it. Dull cramping became the focus of my universe. Turning on the lamp on my bedside table, I lightly explored my belly with my fingertips, feeling the incredible strength of the contracting uterine muscles.

Perhaps I should have been in awe of how perfectly my Maker had planned the process of hormones, stimuli, and indeed, the construction of a woman's body. Instead, my wonder concentrated on the ebb and flow of labor.

It was too soon in the birth process to wake Maurie, but I wanted to share the big news. The remaining hours of night passed at a snail's pace. The rational nurse side of me whispered, "Stay calm. You're not anywhere near ready yet. The pains are still twelve minutes apart. You know first babies take about twelve hours, and your doctor's in the next room!"

Every pregnant woman wants the TV version of labor—the script where, with three stunning pains and intact makeup, a woman's baby is born after two final pushes. Of course, television and movies don't show real pregnancies either—the puffy face, swollen ankles, itchy skin, the half-dozen middle of the night trips to the bathroom. I experienced the reality version.

The frightened girl inside me shouted, "Maurie should know I'm in labor! I need to get to the hospital, don't I? Oh, wake up Pam. I know Maurie had a long day yesterday, but it's time to get him off to work. He can just take me with him to the hospital."

Finally, muffled creaks of the bedsprings and feet thudding on the floor in the next room signaled Maurie getting up. I wanted to scream with relief. I heard the floorboards squeak, heard him pad past my room and close the bathroom door.

When he emerged, I'd opened my door, and he peeked in from the hallway. His face reflected concern as to why my light shone so early.

My grin announced the big news.

He asked me a few questions and went back to his room.

No time for a shower. I threw on my clothes and made the bed.

A half hour later Maurie left for the hospital—without me.

Downstairs, I paced through the morning while Pam performed her usual chores. Eyes glued to my watch, I announced the timing between my contractions. I was certain her next phone consultation with Maurie would direct us to speed to the hospital.

At last, Maurie instructed Pam to drive me in to Buffalo. "You've got plenty of time, Pam. I've given the admissions office her information, and they're expecting her." Pam strolled out her front door with the boys and took them across the street to her parents' home. "I'll just get the boys settled with my mother and be right back. Go ahead and get the car warmed up."

I hurried out the back door to the alley and waited in her black sedan. I barely noticed the sunshine trying to warm the winter's day. I timed two additional contractions, wondering why Pam stayed gone so long. I told myself it seemed long because I was in labor. I still wanted to get to the hospital as soon as possible.

Pam and I pulled up to the hospital entrance at noon. She hugged me good-bye, assuring me, "Maurie's got everything arranged. They'll take you right upstairs." I wanted to beg her to stay with me but kept my mouth clamped shut as another dull pain stomped across my pelvis.

An admissions aide came through the doors as Pam drove away. She helped me into a wheel chair, had me sign a couple of forms, and wheeled me off to labor and delivery. The skinny bed in the labor room stood close to the wall, its end facing the doorway. I tossed and turned with each pain. The sweat-drenched sheets came loose from the foot of the bed. I didn't care whether they covered any part of me. My left elbow rubbed against the textured wall every time I moved.

The nurses stayed busy elsewhere and spoke to me only when they checked my blood pressure and dilation. Maurie came into the room a couple of times and sat beside me on the bed while he assessed my progress.

The afternoon dragged by, interrupted only as my roommates stopped by on their way home after work. Maurie had called them. They didn't stay long.

Shift change brought on another nurse. She didn't hang around to visit either. I heard occasional footsteps in the hall and other people talking somewhere in the distance.

Around four o'clock the nurse came in, probed inside me, and announced, "It's time to start pushing." She showed me how to pull my legs up and watched me through the next contraction. "Atta girl. I'll be back in a little while to see how you're doing." The door closed behind her.

Outside my window, the darkening sky mirrored what lay before me.

I tried not to cry.

. . .

The pains astounded me. Clutching pale white knees, I strained and pushed until it grew dark outside. I wanted to scream.

I wanted someone to hold my hand.

I wanted the pain to end.

I was terrified it would.

I knew my child's delivery would be an abrupt ending to our era—the shared nourishment, warmth, music, history—the ultimate finis.

Once in the cool delivery room, the nurse helped me to a sitting position on the narrow table. She pushed my chin onto my chest as I sat cross-legged, hunched tight over my bulging belly. Maurie worked to administer anesthetic through a saddle block.

It seemed to take forever. Feeling another contraction beginning, I tried not to envision the pressure this position put on my baby, fearing he might somehow be born from this crowded pose.

I attempted to focus on panting, while my mind screamed, "Hurry, Maurie. Get the block in! Please let me push again…"

Several more sharp pinpricks followed. Nursing experience told me Dr. Dewey was having difficulty locating an open space between my vertebrae. Attempting to spread the bones farther apart, the nurse leaned on the back of my head and shoulders and pulled me down into a tighter ball.

Like a wounded bear, I grunted through another contraction. Another pinprick.

Maurie said, "Okay, let's get her down now."

Blessed respite began. The intense pressure vanished. My legs turned to inanimate heavy logs. As though dismembered, I watched in amazement while Maurie and the nurse each lifted a leg and positioned me for delivery. I couldn't feel the cold of the metal stirrups. I couldn't tell how hard I pushed at Maurie's urging for "Now, deep breath, one more good push, Donna. That's a girl. Keep pushing, keep pushing…"

I felt my body pulled toward the end of the table as Maurie guided the baby the last few centimeters through the birth canal. I sensed no pain. Damp with sweat, my teeth chattered as I shook from exhaustion.

I heard a deep cry. Then, another.

I squeezed my eyes shut and began to wither inside.

Chapter Fourteen

Maurie knew I felt I couldn't see my baby.

I felt pressure from a body against my leg in the stirrup and knew the nurse now stood at the foot of the table. She murmured something. Awareness that by this time she'd be holding my baby struck me. Any second she'd bring the baby to the head of the table for me to see. Shaking my head, I squeezed my eyes shut tighter until my ears roared.

"No, don't." I heard urgency in Maurie's voice. "Put him in the incubator, now." His directive prevented her from showing me the baby. It also told me I'd been right all along. She carried my *son*.

By the quick *squish, squish* of her crepe-soled shoes, I knew she rushed past me and took her bundle to the incubator. Resolute, I opened my eyes and fixed them on the far side of the room to be certain I didn't accidentally connect with my child.

I smelled the birth waters. I felt the chilly air and knew it seeped around him across the sterile room. I heard lusty, quavering howls of protest at the change of everything in his existence. Without seeing, I knew his arms flailed and his frantic kicks searched for warm, familiar confinement.

My sweet, sweet baby! I hear you. I know you.

I could swim in his mewling all day, and yet in it, I would drown.

• • •

My heart ripped when I heard his cries recede as his nurse carried him from the area. The swinging door closed with a whoosh of air, and the newborn sounds faded. I opened my eyes. Maurie sat hunched over, focused at his work between my legs.

The cold room grew quiet, tomb-like.

Tears slid down the sides of my face. My shaking became uncontrollable.

I felt more tugging but no pain. *The placenta.* I heard a distinct plop as it landed in a basin.

Maurie stood up from his stool and broke the silence as he pulled down his mask to speak in a quiet, calm voice.

From a million miles away, I watched his lips move. His blue eyes probed mine as though he worried that the rhythm of my soul would spin out of control.

"Donna, you had a boy. He looks fine."

I wanted to board a train that would never stop to let me off.

• • •

A nurse wheeled me to a deserted end of the maternity ward, far from the laughter of new mothers, not far enough from the nursery. On a prescribed post-partum schedule, one of the floor nurses came by to check on me. Each morning and evening, Maurie came as he made his rounds. Pam came for short visits. I wished she'd stay longer, but she said she'd left the boys with her mother and needed to get back home.

Mostly I cried alone. I didn't even talk to God.

Every four hours, I listened as wheels squealed on the linoleum floors outside my room. Workers pushed cribs out of the nursery. Feeding time. The hallway quieted except for the cries of one baby who needed sustenance, love, and holding.

Whatever the hour, my pleas matched those of my son. Both our cries remained trapped in me, echoing inside my head. The torture continued for three full days. My empty, sagging belly matched my deflating spirit. Every four hours around the clock, I heard his solitary crying. Every minute I grieved over his plight.

That's my baby crying in there. Why isn't someone holding him? He needs somebody. Please rock him. Sing to him. He knows so many songs… "Oh Danny Boy, the pipes, the pipes are callin'…"

In the darkest hours before dawn of the third morning, I could no longer stand the torment. I crept out of my room.

As sure as the moon directs the tide, something immutable drew me down the long, dim corridor toward the bright lights of the nursery. I had to see my son.

My coworker looked up and saw me standing in silence before the plate glass window. No words passed between us. She knew what I wanted. She crossed to his Plexiglas crib at the back of the room, held him up, pulled the blanket away from his shoulders.

Tears blurred my vision, but through them I saw rose-pink cheeks and dark, dark hair. Then, and there, God filled the shriveled cavity of my heart with a mother's infinite tenderness. The unmistakable beating against my ribs became a new, exquisite pain.

The nurse placed him back in his crib, came out to the hall, and hugged me in the silent night as I sobbed. "Donna, he's a beautiful baby. I know Dr. Dewey will find him a good home."

I nodded, chilled and numb by sudden cold. "That's the only thing getting me through all this."

My head hung as I focused on the polished floor tiles while I finished the long, slow walk back to my room. I looked in the mirror over the sink and gazed at a pale face with bloodshot eyes and a downcast mouth.

I am alone for the first time in nine months.

All alone.

My son is alone.

• • •

Despite the real-life trial I'd just managed—I thought for the most part by myself—I never felt more of a failure as a woman.

I'd loved working in the nursery just down the hall from my room of exile. Now, I tried to ignore my surroundings. When certain scents wafted my way, they triggered familiar images of shampooed, soft little heads, tender skin covered in pink lotion, even the tiny bottoms swathed with white petroleum jelly to ward off diaper rash.

I reflected how I sang to my charges and how I rocked tiny preemies. My work in the past four months had been more like being a mommy to dozens of infants than like being a nurse. No matter the census, I changed those sweet things lickety-split, swaddled them in soft, flannel blankets, and delivered them to their mommas, right on schedule.

A smaller number of babies in the nursery meant more time to indulge myself in holding each one just a few minutes before and after their feeding times. I'd handled babies every day for months, dressed them in tiny new outfits and blankets, and with love, I'd placed them in their mother's arms for the ride home.

Clinging to the far-off image of unfamiliar, soft hands caressing my baby's pink cheeks, I readied myself for the inevitable. I couldn't recall how this was all supposed to happen. The painful details I once discussed with Maurie now eluded me.

• • •

I lay in bed, feeling hopeless.

A knock on the door...officious-looking papers held out to me.

A stranger in a dark suit and navy tie stood there, smiling, looking uneasy. He said, "Just ring your call-light for a nurse when you're finished."

I took the pen he offered, trying to wipe away the tears, trying to read the words.

Words that pierced my heart like a well-driven nail. *I, Donna Marie Granger, hereby consent to the adoption of the above-named child by...*

I agonized over signing my name. With just the stroke of a pen, and without so much as a whisper of a brush of his angel cheek to mine, I would send my own son into a cold, February day. Bereft of alternatives, it still took hours to sign my name.

Empty, hollow, and defeated, the act of scribbling my signature drained me of my last remaining ounce of courage. Beyond the scratching of the pen, I heard a baby's cries in the distance. My new heart bounced like a pinball around my chest. I found it impossible to react. I just held on.

. . .

I don't know how she did it, but Pam kept me sane when I returned to her home. Perhaps she possessed an innate compassion coupled with her nurse's love of psychiatry. Each day she nourished my mind as well as my body. She didn't discuss the adoption but listened whenever I shared my pain. Despite her duties as a wife and mother, she let me talk as long as I needed.

Nighttime, however, remained grief-filled. In the dark of my bedroom, I dreamed of my child wrapped in a soft, blue blanket. I saw hands reaching into his crib to pick him up, but I couldn't get further into the vision. I awoke and cried into my pillow night after night.

After a few days, I gleaned solace from a sense that Pam and Maurie knew the family adopting my son. I didn't know who they were, but if they were friends of the Deweys, they had to be wonderful people. Still unsure of my decision, I began to pray again. *God, please, please place my baby where he is safe and loved.* Gradually, a certain sense of calm settled about me.

Meanwhile, a few steps away, a life-changing drama unfolded.

. . .

Three weeks after I returned to his home, Maurie found me temporary employment. He recommended me as a private duty nurse for a friend's father who was dying of cancer. My new employer and his wife were a sweet couple, and while I worked, I kept my mind occupied with the details of my patient's care.

I swallowed back the tears always skimming beneath the surface as I filled my aching, empty arms with this frail man.

As my body healed, Pam and I talked, laughed together, and developed a deep friendship. Gentle, sure, and strong, she coaxed me from social withdrawal. I began to find humor in life again.

Appalled by my flabby stomach, I attempted to lose weight. Pam wanted to lose a few pounds herself and talked Maurie into giving us both diet pills. The pills gave us boundless energy, and we completed household chores in record time. They also made it easy to starve ourselves, but much to Maurie's dismay, we didn't drop tons of weight. We both craved sweets and succumbed to hot fudge sundaes when we had company for dinner. While our guests waited at the dining room table, Pam dished out ice cream. I ladled hot fudge and sprinkled on a few pecans. Giving us each an extra portion, Pam said, "I keep telling Maurie we ought to have dinner parties more often."

We cooked side-by-side and entertained with dinners for Maurie's contemporaries and their wives. Like Maurie, they were establishing new practices and juggling large debts of medical school loans, but they had promising futures.

On a Saturday evening after one of her delicious meals, everyone crowded into the kitchen as Pam and I cleaned up. After-dinner talk included topics of which I had no personal experience—huge tax bills, office personnel issues, partnership agreements. The conversation was loud and lively. I remained content to stay quiet and in the background.

I felt Maurie would be discreet about me as a patient. Still, as physicians who all worked at Buffalo General, I felt they must have known of my recent shame. I didn't know how Pam explained my living in their home.

I stood at the sink rinsing dishes when one of the men called out, "Donna?"

I turned toward the group across the kitchen, expecting him to ask for a glass of water, or perhaps more pink Catawba wine.

"How are you feeling?"

I felt the instant heat of humiliation rise to my face. I jerked away mumbling, "Fine." I wished with all my heart that I could follow the water swirling down the drain. I looked at my stomach, still protruding enough to touch the edge of the sink. How I wished I could say to these people, "Please don't judge me. Love me."

He broke the silence with the kindest words I'd heard in a very long time. "Donna, you're not any different than the rest of us. We just didn't get caught."

Stunned to hear murmurs of assent, I turned around in time to see two wives smiling at me and nodding their heads in agreement. My shame lifted. From that moment on, I felt like their equal and looked forward to participating in their conversations.

I knew several of these couples had babies and toddlers at home, but for the most part, they avoided the topic of parenthood. If the subject of a mother's sleepless night or a visit to the pediatrician came up, I instantly went on alert for any hint they'd adopted my baby. I never got any real sense it was any of them. Perhaps not one of these couples, still, I felt certain he was with friends of Pam and Maurie.

After the parties, I went to my room thinking of these young professionals, their wives, and their rosy futures. I wondered if mine could ever be the slightest bit pink.

• • •

Maurie, Pam, and I shared a love of antiques, and Pam and I hunted them as people do who have limited resources. The evening before trash pick up, the curbs of Buffalo always yielded an interesting, albeit dirty or chipped find or two. We bundled the boys into coats over their pajamas, buckled them onto their booster seats, and prowled up and down the streets, slowing beneath streetlights that lit promising piles.

Winters in the northeast bring premature darkness, and on one such shadowy night, while on a foraging expedition, I jumped from the car to grab the pièce de résistance of the evening.

Pam implored me to hurry. "Donna! A car's coming."

I giggled at the possibility of the Buffalo newspaper's next headline, "Doctor's wife seen loading roadside treasures into black Mercedes."

I half-carried, half-dragged a large, three-story martin house toward her car. In my haste, I tripped over spilled trash, sending empty cans and boxes flying with a very loud series of crashes. Still, I managed to haul the unwieldy prize onto my lap and slammed my door shut before the car passed.

"You know, Pam, I'm probably going to get lockjaw from the nails sticking out of this thing. They're digging into my legs right through my pants, and I am *certain* they didn't give me a tetanus shot in the delivery room."

Pam's laugh came out as a snort as she eased the car away from the curb. It felt very good to be able to laugh at myself again. Hiding our faces when headlights approached, we reveled at our ridiculous stealth and headed home. Even more amusing than our sneaking around trash piles in the dark, we seemed to be taking the same route as the car in front of us. When our lights illuminated his car's interior, we noticed the driver taking frequent looks at us in his rearview mirror. Our vehicles made the same turns up and down the streets.

His car sped up.

We kept pace, still behind him.

Suddenly he careened into a driveway ahead, jumped out of his car, and raced to a porch.

Puzzled, Pam and I looked at each other. She glanced in her mirror and burst out laughing.

"Look in the back seat!"

Silhouetted by the streetlight behind us, Pam's boys rode in their favorite outfits, Batman and Robin masks in place. Their unmistakable bat profiles, like the ones in the newest hit movie, *Batman*, sent us into fresh gales of laughter.

• • •

My private duty work ended after my patient succumbed to his cancer. Although I hated to leave Pam and Maurie, I needed to face the world again. An older and wiser Pam knew I wasn't quite ready. Like a big sister, she guided me toward the last step of resolving one of the guilt feelings I stored deep inside. "Donna, you've got to tell your mother. You're too close to keep this from her for the rest of your lives. She needs to know what's happened."

With her encouragement, I called my mother to ask her to get on a bus and come to Buffalo. It took some smooth talking, but I convinced Mom that sane people *did* live in Buffalo in the wintertime.

"I want you to meet my friends, Mom."

Several seconds later, she asked, "Well, how about this summer?"

"No, Mom. I want you to come now. I haven't seen you in ages, and you'll love these people. Besides, they've got great antiques."

That did it. She bought a bus ticket and came a few days later.

As predicted, she liked Maurie and Pam, adored their sons, and loved their antiques. Watching their youngest son holding a storybook close to his face, she pronounced he needed glasses. His visit to an eye doctor proved her right.

Stalling the moment of disclosure, I took her to see a musical that had just opened at a new big-screen theater in downtown Buffalo. Despite the majestic scenery and beautiful songs of *The Sound of Music*, I focused on the plot of another young woman who wrestled with her personal convictions.

When Mom and I returned from the movies, Pam and Maurie made a discreet exit. It became a full-Kleenex-box night as I told her about the past ten months, and of my rescue by Maurie and Pam. I'll never forget the stricken look on her face.

"Why didn't you tell me, honey?" Tears spilling, she gathered me in her arms. "I know I couldn't make any decisions for you, but it's terrible you had to be alone. I could have been there to talk to."

Always my momma, she let me know she would be just that for-ever, and all the love that statement implied filled my emptiness. At least for a time.

Chapter Fifteen

Sometimes when dreams die, you have to live on with what's left. I picked up my chin, explored a few options, and began a new job. Late that spring, I became one of two nurses for a Girl Scout summer camp in western New York. Being responsible for the health concerns of a large number of scouts with the nearest physician ten miles away made for a challenging but healing summer.

On the far side of the camp, my contemporary began her third summer as head nurse. She lived in a sturdy cabin with two bedrooms, heat, a shower, and an office. I had two cabins, each with three screened and one solid wall. The first cabin came furnished with two cots and two straight-backed chairs.

After surveying my "what to bring to camp" checklist, I'd jammed an old pine washstand from Mom's garage into the Bluebird's cargo area. It served as a small dresser/nightstand. I shared this cabin with another seasoned staffer—an artistic, likeable girl.

The second cabin served as the "sick bay" and held two cots, a rudimentary desk, and a bookshelf. Breezy quarters at best, both cabins stayed damp and moldy. Few rays of sunshine reached their interiors, and a blowing rain invariably found our bedding, clothing, and books. Light bulbs dangling from a long wire in the center of the room lit each cabin. Swinging in the evening wind, they cast dancing shadows about the screens and ceiling.

A long uphill walk yielded a communal staff shower, bathroom, and the large dining hall where our side of the camp met for meals.

There weren't enough counselors to oversee each table, so those of us on auxiliary staff rotated to eat at different tables each meal.

For the most part, I enjoyed being a camp nurse. Staff administrators encouraged us to visit with the scouts and expected us each to be exemplary models for these young women. In my secret heart, I didn't feel like much of a stand-up example—in fact, I felt very small.

Still, I longed for company, and I frequented the campers' tent areas in the evenings. I read A. A. Milne's *Winnie the Pooh* in the smoke-scented firelight. I took on the characters' voices and relayed some of Milne's marvelous life lessons about how one's attitude affects his outcomes. I loved doing bounce-around Tigger and the forlorn Eeyore. The teenagers around me forgot their fifteen-year-old fantasies, record players, and boyfriends as they clamored, "Just one more chapter, please."

I shared my sorrow with my cabin mate one night when she heard me crying into my pillow. In the darkness, I told her of my emptiness and yearning for the thumps I once felt under my heart. "I wish I knew where he was. I need to know someone loves him."

We couldn't see one another, and she said nothing, but I felt she heard me.

I tried again to engage her. "I wonder if he hates me."

She didn't answer. In the morning, camp life resumed for both of us and I never spoke about my grief or its cause again.

I learned new scouting skills and utilized practical nursing a great deal. I kept busy day and evening. Bit by bit, I let go of my sadness. By Labor Day, I'd collected my entire summer's pay of less than $550, packed, and begun the drive toward home to visit Mom. One chapter of my life ended as another opened.

• • •

Conflicting thoughts collided in my head as I drove east along the New York State Thruway. I looked forward to a new life, new relationships—something separate from everything I'd experienced before. Each click of the odometer sent me farther away from Buffalo, closer to a new future. I feared losing the warmth I felt with Pam, as well as the security and sureness of my beloved Maurie.

Did I want to live and work in Glens Falls? Would people sense I had a secret? It'd been four years since I lived at home. How would my family feel about me coming back? I couldn't envision living with my mother—she had her own life, friends, and work. The world seemed to close in on me, and I didn't want to be alone. Each thump of the tires hitting seams in the road amplified the divergence in my mind.

I'd dated a few times over the spring and summer, but I shied away from any hint of intimacy. Would I ever find someone to trust again? I glanced into the rearview mirror. I looked the same but felt tainted, soiled, stained. Could any man ever love me again?

Where would I work? I'd not considered nursing opportunities since early in my senior year of nursing school. I loved working in the nursery and found the care of newborns challenging if one was premature or ill, yet mundane when all went well. The idea of holding another newborn brought great fear. A baby's soft skin, its sweet smell, or its plaintive cry might be enough to carry me over the cliff I edged.

As I reached the tri-city area, I chose an exit, skirted around Albany, and turned north. The towns I passed through looked old and worn, their houses packed together on city streets laid out more than a century earlier. The last hour of the drive filled me with dread, anticipation, sadness, and excitement.

I turned in the driveway and honked the horn as I rounded the corner of the brick house I knew so well. My mother, bent over the stone wall of her garden, looked up at me with her familiar smile. I was home.

• • •

Between jobs herself, Mom and I decided to take a vacation trip to California. I planned to work along the way, and Mom hoped to find a few nanny jobs once we got to her brother's outside of Los Angeles. We'd stop midway across the country to see my brother Dave on the Texas Gulf Coast. We pooled our resources, purchased AAA route maps, loaded my car, and headed out that fall.

Two women traveling a long distance for an indeterminate length of time probably over-packed. The '65 Mustang Fastback has a skinny rear seat/fold-down cargo deck. With both winter and warm weather clothing, loafers, heels, and sneakers, toiletries, and a cooler for food and drinks, the Bluebird was loaded to the roof.

Since she didn't drive, Mom served as navigator. It didn't take long to discover her rather cavalier attitude about her role. She much preferred watching the passing scenery to studying maps or scanning upcoming route signs.

On the first day out we wore travel clothes—wool skirts and sweaters, nylons—our thighs encased in unyielding Lycra panty girdles. As we sped along the New York State Thruway, I daydreamed a little until Mom scared me half to death. Out of the blue, she shrieked, "Stopppp!" in her very loudest, cardiac arrest causing, high-pitched voice.

Once she admitted to not having an actual emergency, I pulled over as soon as I could and brought the car to a halt. Cars whizzed by as I watched my mother disregard the snagging weeds and scramble down an embankment to gather an armload of pretty but very thorny thistle. I opened the hatchback and waited while she shoved aside clothing to make room for a few dozen jagged stalks. She ignored clumps of dirt spilling from their long roots and slammed the lid closed.

"Honey, it'll look beautiful when it's mixed with dried hydrangea and bittersweet!" As long as I could remember, she'd delighted in making handsome arrangements designed for her pewter coffee pots. Multiple runs in her hosiery and trailing scratches on her legs evidenced the lengths she'd gone to obtain this wondrous flora.

This is on the way to *California.*

Speeding along again, Mom waved at truckers seated high above us in their big rigs. When we passed these gallant drivers, they flicked their lights to signal we'd cleared their vehicles' huge front ends. A string of eighteen-wheelers often sandwiched us in between when rain or snow limited visibility.

As often as possible, I took less traveled routes. I wanted to get a feel for the people and towns along the way. The trip became a time of bonding for my mother and me. Traveling, seeing the nooks and crannies of off-the-beaten path America together, and enjoying a few double dinner dates on the way excited us.

. . .

The day after our arrival at Dave's house, I found temporary employment at a nearby hospital. A few weeks later, my brother introduced me to my future husband. With a handsome face and beautiful white teeth, Don spoke in a long, delicious Texas drawl. He had a soft laugh and exuded welcome, easy warmth.

On a parkway edging my brother's home, Don and I strolled along after our first date, held hands, and talked until dawn. I found him to be a good listener, and to my own amazement, I told him about my pregnancy and decisions about my son. When I lamented meeting him after the fact, he displayed a sweet tenderness and held me close. At sunrise, he told me he wanted to marry me. I knew things were moving too fast but promised I'd consider marriage as Mom and I continued our trip.

Two days later, Don took Mom and me to a fabulous restaurant in Houston for lunch. Beside our table, a waiter in a crisp white jacket dressed my huge caesar salad in the largest bowl I'd ever seen. Even my father would approve of Don's perfect table manners as he cut his steak and laid the knife across the edge of his plate. After he paid the check, Don popped a toothpick into his mouth, and working it between his teeth with one hand, opened the door for us to leave. I'd never seen anyone pick his teeth in public. Aghast, I asked, "You're not going to leave that in your mouth outside, are you?"

"Well," he drawled, "would you rather I talked to y'all with straings of meat hangin' from my teeth?"

Welcome to Texas, girls.

The next day Mom and I still laughed about it as we I headed west again toward my aunt and uncle's home in California.

I worked at a new hospital north of Los Angeles where the pay scale was double what I'd made in New York. Eager to earn enough to finance our eventual trip home, I worked a day shift, followed by a private duty shift until eleven p.m. On my days off, my aunt and uncle took Mom and me to visit Disney Land, Knott's Berry Farm, and Catalina Island.

Two single coworkers showed me California nightlife. I'd missed the carefree "now I have a good job and money to spend" time after graduation, and I determined I'd make up for it. Sleep didn't seem important—I felt young and alive for the first time in more than a year.

Even with California's liberal culture, I felt I couldn't talk about my recent history. If I revealed my secret, how would my aunt and uncle view me? If no longer considered a "good girl," could I still be a favorite niece? During her visits over the holidays, I loved rocking their ten-month-old granddaughter. I couldn't seem to stop seeking the sweet torture of holding and singing to little Holly. Thinking about another baby the same age, I kissed her dark hair a hundred times.

Envelopes, addressed in Don's precise handwriting arrived in the mail every morning. I read a few parts to my mother but kept much of the contents private. Our whirlwind courtship that began in Texas bloomed through hundreds of long-distance phone calls and our love-declaring letters.

One evening, Don asked me to describe my vision of an engagement ring. I mumbled something about liking round-cut stones. Like night owls picking up the scrambling of a distant field mouse,

Mom and my aunt zoomed in on the topic of our nearby conversation. They butted in to add their own two cents' worth. Loud enough for him to hear, my aunt said, "She'd like a platinum setting, of course." To my total embarrassment, my mother added, "You'd better make it a good-sized diamond, Don. She's got long fingers."

Thankfully, Don laughed. "Okay, okay, girls. I get the picture."

I promised to meet him in Dallas as we passed through Texas on our way home again.

• • •

Driving our loaded car home proved even more challenging than our trip west. Somehow, we'd crammed an astonishing number of additional odd items into the shrinking space behind the bucket seats. To our snazzy pink, lime green, and turquoise California outfits, we added Christmas presents from my aunt and uncle, an antique sixteen-inch stoneware vinegar pig, and a large, flat box holding a new wedding gown and veil. Following Don's directions in his last letter, I drove into the maze of streets in downtown Dallas.

About the time my son was seeing his first birthday candle in western New York, my mother and I pulled into the designated Italian restaurant. Never one to delay a meal, she'd already started to worry. "I wonder how long we'll have to wait for Don. I'm starving."

"Don't worry, Mom. He knows how long it takes to drive here. Let's find the restroom and get a table."

Before we could climb out of the car, Don arrived and parked next to us.

We made small talk after placing our orders. Don excused himself and went to the restroom. He appeared nervous—perhaps because he didn't know my mother very well.

We ate our salads. My mother emptied most of the breadbasket. When she ran out of butter, she put her knife down on the table with a thud. "I can't stand it one more minute. Let's see the ring."

I wanted to slide under the table and right out the front door. Before I could run, however, our waitress approached with a tray piled high with our dinners. Her eyes lit on Don as he pulled a small blue velvet box out of his coat pocket.

She must have realized what was taking place, and in her excitement, she dumped a full plate of hot spaghetti onto his lap.

Despite his pain—and my fleeting but very real concern whether or not we'd ever have children—Don proposed. A one-carat brilliant-cut diamond sparkled from its blue velvet box. Proud and dazzled by the exhilaration of it all, I accepted and rode the rest of the way back to New York on cloud nine.

• • •

Mom and I had traveled for four months and covered almost seven thousand miles. We'd shared many adventures. Most important to me, we now loved one another as adult mother-daughter-friends. She accepted that I'd be moving to Texas, but she didn't want me to rush into marriage. Particularly to a man I'd known by telephone and mail and only dated three times. The closer we got to home, the more she begged me to get to know Don better before we married.

Trying another tactic, she pleaded, "At least wait until the weather is warm and the snow's gone."

Visions of a summer wedding were hers, not mine. Don and I wanted to end our long-distance engagement and begin married life together.

• • •

Mom, Dale, and I threw together an April wedding guest list, at Don's request arranged the ceremony at a Lutheran church, and planned the reception at an area dude ranch. Don came a few days beforehand to meet the rest of my family. Asking Dale to be his best man touched off a series of catastrophes.

On Thursday, we met the pastor for counseling. Fuming that my father didn't show for the wedding rehearsal, I allowed Dale to take my arm and march me toward a Lutheran pastor none of us knew. The pastor Don and I met with stayed at home with shingles. As we finished the last run-through, Dad banged open the church doors and staggered toward us down the aisle.

Dale whispered, "I can't believe he's drunk."

I couldn't either.

Clutching a pew, Dad gasped out that a drunk driver had rear-ended his car in front of the church. His back in painful spasms, we sent my father off to the emergency room.

Twice that next morning, the honest-to-goodness FBI detained and questioned our best man. A police sketch on television looked enough like Dale to prompt a number of people to call and identify him as the bank robber they sought.

My California wedding gown, a long candlelight silk sheath with a simple train, made me feel elegant. After the ceremony, the wedding party posed for the photographer as our guests proceeded on to the reception, ten miles away. Mom's fears about the weather affecting our wedding turned valid. Water spots dotted my gown and shoes as Don and I exited the church to soft snowflakes swirling in the night. It was snowing hard by the time our limo passed a number of cars stopped on the side of the road.

When we arrived at the dude ranch, the limo driver pulled under the covered entryway—inches behind a state police car with its lights flashing. Sick to my stomach at yet another embarrassing intrusion into the happiest day of a girl's life, I flew out of the limo door. Veil flying around me, I raced into the lobby and headed straight for a uniformed trooper.

"You are not arresting my brother! He's the best man at my wedding, and I need…" Bursting into tears, I clutched the startled man's arm.

Wedding guests milling in the lobby stopped all conversation and stared. Pale and worried looking, Don appeared and gently removed my hand from the trooper's arm.

"Lady, lady," the officer stammered, "I just followed a speeder in here and gave him a ticket."

A groomsman told us later that one of our guests' cars had hit a horse on the freeway, and several other cars in the procession collided to avoid hitting it again. In spite of all this calamity and the fact that Dad's back spasms made him lurch more than glide about when we danced our father-daughter dance, I managed to enjoy my wedding.

. . .

Don and I left Glens Falls the next morning. I wondered when I'd see my parents again. The Bluebird held our suitcases and towed a small U-Haul trailer filled with wedding gifts, a few of Mom's antiques, my large, round aqua hairdryer, and the red radio.

On our way to Texas, we honeymooned in Washington, DC. When we called my mother from our hotel, she told us they'd caught the bank robber. He didn't look anything like his sketch aired on television—or anything like Dale.

I wrote to Pam and Maurie on hotel stationery, describing our big day and honeymoon trip, never guessing the Washington return address could later cause much confusion and frustration.

Don and I lived in Lake Jackson, a beautiful city where the foliage stayed a perpetual green because of its proximity to the warm Texas Gulf Coast. He worked for a large chemical company. Despite the fear of being alone with a woman in labor, fainting in the operating room, as well as the predictions of noninterest that the gynecologist expressed while I was a student nurse, I worked in an ob-gyn practice. I loved working with pregnant women, and I now assisted at most of our surgeries.

With both of us eager to start our family, it didn't take long for me to conceive. Several weeks after the pregnancy's confirmation, it became obvious things weren't progressing. I told myself everything would be okay because I felt fine.

On a Friday afternoon almost two months later, in a rush of fluids, I miscarried while at work. As an obstetrical nurse, I knew many doctors considered miscarriages blessings in disguise, as these fetuses often had birth defects. I didn't feel blessed—I felt very sorry for myself. I stayed in bed rather than go to church that Sunday.

Once back to my familiar routine, I spent my days surrounded by pregnant women. At their deliveries, I presented them with their new babies. I smiled at work, but bedtime brought the familiar nightmare back from seventh grade. Night after night, I tossed and turned in bed, feeling lost and insecure, unable to find my own way. Added to the old nightmare, a sobbing little boy with dark hair held his arms out and trailed after me. How I longed to wear my mother's kind of smile as she reminisced about holding me in her arms as an infant.

CHAPTER SIXTEEN

"You're not going to cry this time, right?"

My new employer, Dr. Ron Paul, and I stood side by side at the surgical sinks, scrubbing for a delivery. His question was half in jest. He knew what happened each time he handed me a slippery, wriggling newborn.

"Nope, I'm not going to cry."

I always promised not to cry, but I broke each pledge. The pure miracle of a new baby did me in every time.

From his first day in the office, this boyishly handsome young physician demonstrated a clear respect for women and a love of babies. He worked in the delivery room and surgery with great compassion and sure, efficient technical expertise.

I worked hard for Dr. Paul, and in a short while, he promoted me to office manager. He also became my doctor. As he reviewed my medical history, I told him about my first pregnancy. He listened without much comment. Having witnessed my tears of wonder and joy at deliveries, he must have known I shared his love for babies. I believed he surmised what it cost me to do what I thought was right for my own.

Many of our patients requested I come to the hospital when they went into labor. Dr. Paul allowing me to deliver their baby while he stood beside me thrilled me. Holding a newborn and handing it to its mother delighted me as much the one hundredth time as the first. Thrust into the scents, sounds, and drama of dozens of deliveries, I longed for a baby I didn't have to hand to another woman.

God answered my prayers, and Don and I rejoiced over our son Jonathan, born early one morning in December 1969. At last, I had my own sweet baby boy to nurse, to rock, to sing to sleep. Six weeks later, my maternity leave ended. I went back to work, leaving Jonathan in the care of a devoted nanny. As much as I loved my job, I couldn't wait to get home from work to cuddle my son.

Jonathan was a blond-haired, blue-eyed two-year-old when I gave birth to our daughter on a Friday night in September. A few weeks premature, Stephanie became gravely ill within hours of her birth. As she struggled through hours of rapid respirations, fever, and then pneumonia, her weight dropped precipitously.

Bedridden with post-partum phlebitis, I couldn't nurse her or even visit her. Don paced the hallway in front of the nursery windows. My mother came from New York. We dreaded each of the pediatrician's reports, "I'm sorry, but her weight dropped again—she's lost more than half a pound. Her lungs are congested, and her temperature's still up."

By the fourth day, the pediatrician told us our daughter baby was at a critical juncture. Our pastor visited, and I nodded my head in miserable agreement, consenting for him to baptize baby Stephanie. I clung to my belief that God *would not* let her die. I wrestled with thoughts of a just God, a righteous God, a loving God. In the end, I still didn't trust in Him.

Although it meant risking a clot tearing loose from my inflamed leg vein, I begged to be present for her baptism. With my mother and Don's on either side of me, I sat in a wheelchair and watched as the pastor tilted back the top of the incubator and slid her toward him. The nursery window muted his incantations.

The last time I'd seen my baby, we were still in the delivery room. Even before the nurse wiped her clean, her skin glowed a remarkable pink color as she waved her arms and legs in quick little jerks. Her vigorous cries echoed across the tiled walls. Now she lay still and thin, panting like a dog on an August afternoon. Reports of her one-hundred-ten respirations a minute came to life before me, as shattering as a slap in the face. Each time her tiny rib cage rose and fell, her breastbone seemed to sink to her spine. A tiny soft black mask shielded her delicate eyes from the oxygen flooding the incubator.

Pastor droned on. I stared in horror as my baby, without benefit of oxygen, became progressively grayer. It was all I could do to stay seated. I promised God I would never fail in my duty as a mother again if He let her live. At last, he seemed to mouth "amen" and step aside. The nurse adjusted Stephanie and her tubes inside the safety of her incubator.

I looked up at Don's mother to ask for a Kleenex. Her eyes streamed tears as her lips moved in soft prayer. She hadn't brought a tissue. Although she needed one too, my mother didn't have one. I clung to Mom's hand as Don's mother steered my wheelchair back to my room.

Respiratory distress syndrome in infants can end as suddenly as it begins. God answered my prayer and provided another miracle. I took my pinked-up baby home the next morning.

Four weeks later at her second baptism, I stood at the front of the church looking down at Stephanie's dark hair, beautiful blue eyes, and pink cheeks. Preoccupied in his toddler's world, Jonathan clung to his father's legs beside me. He had yet to pay Stephanie much attention.

Somewhere, I have another little boy who has dark hair and pink cheeks. He's six now. I wonder if he'd like having a new baby sister.

Serving as godparents, Ron and his wife, Carol, stood nearby to join us in thanking God for His blessings.

• • •

The same loving woman who'd cared for Jonathan for the past two years continued to come to our home while I worked. My house stayed clean, Jonathan and Stephanie thrived, and although I worked ten- and eleven-hour days, Don and I lived what I considered a happy life.

Every evening I came home from work, fed my family, and bathed the children. In their room afterward, I sat and read a nighttime storybook. Lingering shampoo perfumes in their hair brought back the scents of my hospital nursery days. After they fell asleep, I left the house to begin my second job, cleaning the office.

Don and I both wanted the best for Jonathan and Stephanie, and as their world expanded with outside activities, we became involved parents. As each new season's photos were developed, we marveled at the speed at which our children grew.

I had no control over the thoughts that caused me to pause in the middle of our busy lives. In the solitude of church, during the hubbub of Christmas mornings, every Mother's Day, and most often each February, I thought about another boy growing up somewhere far away. Was he safe? Did his parents love him?

All the while, life marched past me like a passing parade.

• • •

My work world changed in the mid-seventies, when Dr. Paul entered the harsh world of politics. He campaigned for a position as a US Congressman.

His writings and speeches left no doubt of his belief in less government, adherence to the Constitution, and fear for our nation's economy. A man of strong faith, Ron became an eloquent spokesperson for individual liberty, as well as that of the unborn.

I cried for three days at the thought of him leaving his medical practice. It took a while, but I learned to love the new facets of this strong man. I wrote a check to kick off his grassroots campaign, hosted a coffee social, and progressed to knocking on doors with him on our days off. I listened and watched his passion for liberty excite people to learn and think for themselves. I became a devoted follower, unabashedly proud to know and work with him.

As a US Representative, Ron wanted to be available to his Texas district constituents. For years, he assisted in surgery on Monday mornings, caught a plane to Washington by late morning, and returned home to Texas on Thursday nights.

I also committed myself as a busy community volunteer and served in our Junior Service League teaching CPR. I attended civic and charity board meetings, chaired events, sang in our church choir, and taught Sunday school. I hungered after the pleasurable feeling of belonging.

I continued to work hard at managing the medical practice for Ron and his partner, took continuing education courses, and stayed active in nursing organizations. I loved my career and craved success on a personal level, as well as for the practice.

A high percentage of professionals lived in our wealth-driven community, and keeping up with the Joneses remained a challenge. Stinging memories of a wardrobe of two dresses in seventh grade and no money for the superfluous possessions my peers enjoyed, I felt a duty to provide material things for my children. While most of my friends were working mothers who held eight- or nine-hour-a-day teaching jobs, I added bookkeeping and preparing allergy shot mixes for another physician to my evening office cleaning chores.

Jonathan and Stephanie were involved in a number of grade school extracurricular activities. Despite working two and sometimes three jobs, I threw myself into the efforts of being a good mom, missing few soccer games, scouting activities, church, or school events. I attended League meetings and socials, charity outings, and fundraising events for Ron.

Don immersed himself in scouting and soccer. He and Jonathan spent many weekends camping and enjoying the camaraderie of first Cub, then Boy Scout outdoor life. With his dad's encouragement, Jonathan worked diligently on his merit badges. While "the boys" camped, Stephanie and I kept the home fires burning and enjoyed each other's company.

Somehow, I found my long work hours redemptive; I never questioned whether I could be a truly good wife, mother, employee, and busy volunteer all at the same time.

· · ·

My husband struggled to be comfortable in the midst of strangers our entire married life, but by the late seventies, I no longer begged him to attend social or political events. He assured me he didn't mind staying at home; and rather than remain by his side, I went alone. Something had to give, and it shames me to admit now that I became so involved with my work and volunteer activities I allowed my marriage to disintegrate.

For three years, I spiraled headfirst into a self-made chaos. I considered a divorce but dreaded its possible effects on our children, especially Jonathan, who was as close to his dad as I'd been to mine. I sought counseling for an obscure illusion of a happy marriage. I ached for a resolution to what I deemed societal widowhood.

When I asked Don to join me for counseling, he said I needed to heal from the inside out. By now, I felt so devoid of commitment that my emotional withdrawal worsened the problems for both of us. The counseling I received didn't seem to help, and I felt very much alone. Still, I stuck it out another year. At last, failing to find any value in our marriage, I wounded a very good man by divorcing him.

Learning from the pain of my parents' divorce, I did what I could to salve the inevitable wounds inflicted on my children. Although I wanted to leave Texas and return to New York, I promised my children not to move away, access to their dad whenever they wished, and that I'd spend as much time as I could with each of them.

To Don's everlasting credit, he kept a quiet dignity and made the transition through a difficult year easier for all of us. He took Jonathan, Stephanie, and me along as he hunted for a nearby rental so the children could ride their bikes to visit him. We vowed never to let our feelings interfere with our commitment as parents, and despite my attorney's professional advice to the contrary as not in my best interest, we shared his services, as well as the children's custody. Don is still a wonderful father and a comfortable friend.

Even though I had a steady job and child support from Don, I experienced the stunning loneliness and overwhelming responsibility of a single mom with two children. Although I'd worked two jobs for more than fifteen years, I had no credit in my own name. It frightened me.

In our phone conversations, I often acknowledged my mother's bravery. "Mom, I don't know how you did it without a career to fall back on."

"Well, honey, you do the best you can, and you keep on working at whatever job you can find until you can climb out of the hole, no matter who dug it."

Licking a stamp for the last of the bill payment envelopes, I dialed Mom's number. Despite my tight finances, I refused to cut back on calls to her. I could just see her knowing smile when I told her I needed to conserve electricity and had determined we could do without air conditioning until Memorial Day. Temperatures along the Texas Gulf Coast rose steadily that spring. By early May, when the children and I arrived home in the late afternoons, the house thermostat read ninety-five degrees. I made us picnic suppers, and we ate outdoors.

Chapter Seventeen

I'd known Ron's brother Wayne for ten years. He was very much like Ron—kind and intelligent with a generous spirit. We dated during the summer of 1982. One evening after a seafood dinner, we strolled along the beach. The sun slipped low on the horizon, and Wayne stood close behind me while we paused to watch the ocean. As his arms encircled me, I leaned my head back on his shoulder. I told this sweet man of my first pregnancy. He didn't say anything for several minutes.

Afraid of this reaction, I turned about to face him. As I disclosed the soft emptiness I still carried, I saw his blue eyes fill. Rather than comment, he gathered me closer and gave me a long, tender kiss on the neck.

We married at the end of summer.

Despite the tears I couldn't suppress at various times over more than three decades, each of these men—Don, Wayne, and Ron—demonstrated patience when I wondered aloud how my dark-haired child fared. Each in his own way tried to be of comfort and offered solace for a situation and an act of submission to the unalterable realities of 1966. It meant a great deal to me to voice my thoughts aloud. Their displays of compassion felt like sturdy knotted ropes extended while I fought the quicksand of my memories.

They also influenced my spirituality. Each of them seemed to possess a serene Christianity that I longed for—an unshakable faith. I wanted the peace of church to last beyond Sunday. My irregular, unstructured prayers rambled through a variety of selfish requests.

The majority of which were the most improbable for me to see answers realized. "Please, God, let my child be safe and healthy. Let him know he is loved."

As time marched on, I spoke less often of my anguish; I knew no one could do anything. It remained my own private moment of hell when I allowed myself the luxury of asking "what if" or "where is" my child.

The days and laws of the sixties moved inexorably onward, but a part of me remained rooted therein. Adoptions were sealed and final; no information released. I had no further rights to my issue. I felt honor-bound to the agreement I'd signed. For all those years, I cried, wondered, and prayed, but I never searched.

• • •

After my divorce, introspection about my marriage to Don sadly revealed how much I'd ignored and neglected in my role as his wife. I took him for granted and did not appreciate what we had—each other, our extended families, and our two beautiful children. I finally figured it out—to have a lasting, fulfilling marriage, I needed to expend a good deal more effort on my spousal relationship. Over the next twenty years, I worked hard at being a good wife, helpmate, and supporter of my husband. As my reward, my love for Wayne has grown deeper each year.

The fact that both my husbands and my children seemed to enjoy my mother's company blessed us all. Escaping New York's long winters, she came and stayed with us each year. As she aged, her visits lengthened until 1993 when she moved to our home in Lake Jackson.

Mom loved Lake O' the Pines almost as much as Wayne and I. Looking like the Clampetts of *The Beverly Hillbillies*, we loaded our pickup truck one weekend a month to ferry household items to the lake house. As money and time off from my job as administrator of an assisted-living community permitted, we added a suite to our lake house for her. We furnished it with some favorite pieces shipped from her home in New York, and eagerly anticipated retirement so we could move there.

In her eighties and still active, horrific pain from a stubborn case of shingles brought my mother to her knees. I hired a compassionate caregiver to stay with her for a few hours a day. For six months, the slightest movement, even the breeze from a ceiling fan, caused her great pain. Forced inactivity led to her becoming bedridden and in need of full-time care, so I left my job of assisting others' parents. Through it all, Mom never lost pride in her appearance, her appetite, or her great attitude. Even as her body wasted until her ribs and hipbones protruded, she kept us laughing. One day after a bath, I put on a fresh diaper and reached for a clean gown. Mom patted her sunken belly, raised a spindly leg up in the air and said, "Just call me Gandhi."

During the three years I cared for my mother, I enjoyed the privilege of long reminisces, reaffirmations of our love for one another, and ample time to say good-bye. Whether ensuring she had a fresh flower from the yard, three home-cooked meals a day, beautiful nighties, or preventive measures to avoid bedsores, I never took a moment with her for granted. I whispered my last good-bye into her ear when she was ninety-three years old. Wayne and I moved to the lake a few months later.

As much as I loved being a wife, I'd always experienced a special joy in my role as a mother. Now that Jonathan and Stephanie lived elsewhere on their own, when I found myself missing them, I worried about all three of my children.

I've never been one to embrace negativity or gloom. Yet here, in the middle of my life, a piece of me died inside each time I thought about my first-born. Though less often now, conjured images of him still came with sharp intensity. Like acid, they etched the chamber in my heart where I held him. I ached for the comfort that might come from knowing what happened after the chapter filled with my baby's adoption ended.

Chapter Eighteen

My mother taught me two essential skills: to cook well and to greet even hard times with a smile and determination. Although my life hadn't been considered a charmed one, I finally became content enough to look forward, even anticipate each tomorrow. People enjoyed my food, and I thought of myself as an ordinary sixty-year-old woman—until I listened to a short book on tape in February 2004.

Perusing the shelves in a bookstore one day, something nagged in a corner of my thoughts. I read the jacket of a popular book about a man in the Bible—Jabez—and his prayer. The book promised great things to those who prayed Jabez's four-line prayer. I'd received many e-mails with such guarantees—provided, of course, I forwarded them to ten friends within an allotted amount of time, along with assurances of "it works!" I may have sent on a couple, but I often hit the delete key. The blurb that caught my attention promised this one daily prayer could help me leave the past behind.

Feeling Wayne could enjoy it too, I bought Thom Lemmons' audio version, *Jabez*, to listen to in the car. The book impressed me. I began a new morning ritual of praying, "Lord, bless me. Expand my territory, keep me from evil, and work Your will through my hands."

I longed to live my life more honestly, more in faith, more in the way Christ taught. *If God blesses me more, if I spread my deeds and efforts farther from home, if I keep away from harmful places and ideas, I might become a better Christian.* Whether by my shift in focus, or God's answer, it soon became easier to live the prayer.

I spoke to more strangers, smiled often, and tried to be interested, rather than interesting. I performed random acts of kindness—picking up litter, mopping up spills on restroom countertops, and the most fun thing, paying for the car behind me at tollbooths. I felt better for helping someone, and each time I shared even the simplest kindness, my delight lasted for days.

The tollbooth fun proved contagious, and soon Wayne explained to perplexed booth operators that we hoped the next person would pass a free toll on to someone else one day. As we pulled forward, we watched in our side mirrors as grinning attendants explained to those behind us they didn't have to pay. We seldom let anyone catch up to us afterward—we weren't after acknowledgement or thanks.

I prayed the prayer of Jabez every day for the rest of February. Then, sure enough, great things started to happen.

It began one evening that March when I drove to the post office near Wayne's office. Even though I usually went inside, it was almost six o'clock, so I opted for the more convenient outside boxes. I eased my car into the drop-off lane behind a woman depositing her mail, and as I waited, I noticed an envelope beneath her vehicle. When she pulled away, I picked up what I thought was her letter. Black tire marks covered the back of the torn envelope. I turned it over and read the address of my husband's accounting firm. I felt my mouth drop open.

When I got home, I handed it to Wayne. "Here, I picked up your mail."

Wayne tore what was left of the envelope open and pulled out a check for $875. He recognized the name on the check, grabbed a phone book, and dialed his client's home.

The client who'd written the check was stunned. "Well, yes, Wayne, I put an envelope in the mailbox for you about noontime today. I dropped a few pieces of my mail by the box, but I thought I'd picked them all up."

He hung up the phone, grinned, and waved the check at me. "What are the odds you wouldn't go into the post office to deposit our mail? Or that you'd notice a piece of mail under the car in front of you? What're the odds it would be addressed to me, honey, and of *you* finding it?"

We smiled bigger at each other—far too many aspects indicated this was a blessing, not luck.

In April, we stopped our truck on the side of Highway 155 so I could gather items that had just blown out of the truck bed. I slid off the seat into an unmown area, taking care to watch where my foot landed, keeping an eye out for snakes. Deep in the grass a few inches from my shoe laid a folded up twenty-dollar bill, water stained and bleached by the sun, but in one piece. That Sunday a faded, folded twenty enlarged our usual church offering.

A month later, I found what appeared to be a rather expensive watch in a restaurant parking lot and turned it in to management. The handsome watch was undamaged. I hoped its owner reclaimed it.

In all these incidents, I didn't believe for a minute in my luck; I knew I was receiving blessing after blessing. I continued my prayer—not from habit or seeking tangible gifts, or even ascribing these blessings to a book on the subject, but because for the first time in my life, I felt the *need* to pray.

And as a result, I found that every now and then extraordinary things *do* happen to ordinary people.

On June 17, 2004, God's grace brought me the most tremendous blessing of all.

•   •   •

The phone rang, breaking the velvet silence of a cool, spring evening. I set my book aside and began the race to answer the kitchen phone before the machine picked up. The route to the phone in my house is always fraught with obstacles—sleeping dogs, discarded shoes, an occasional laundry basket. This night was no exception.

A bit breathless but triumphant, I grabbed the receiver seconds before the fourth ring, "Hello?"

"Is this Donna Paul?" a young voice asked.

"Yes."

"Oh, good. My name is Sarah Herlihy. Um, do you remember Pam Dewey?"

"Of course I remember Pam!"

I haven't spoken to Pam in ages. I quickly figured more than thirty-five years had passed since I'd heard from her, and immediate worry flooded my world. *After all this time, could a phone call mean anything but bad news?*

"Is she all right?"

Sarah chuckled. "Oh, yeah, she's fine. Pam's my mom. She's been searching for you forever, and I offered to help find you. She's missed you and always felt terrible because she lost track of you."

I'd written letters to Pam and Maurie after I left Buffalo, telling them about my travels, that I'd met Don, and all about our long-distance relationship and engagement. I invited them to our wedding. Although they couldn't attend, I'd saved them one of our wedding portraits as a Christmas present. I'd sent them a post card while we spent a few days in Washington, DC. When Don and I settled into our Texas apartment, I wrote a couple more times, but I didn't receive any reply.

Somehow, married life got in the way, heartrending memories faded, and as even the most wonderful friends sometimes do, Pam eased to the back of my mind.

For the next few minutes, Sarah answered my questions about Pam and Maurie, filling me in on their children, adopted kids (one of whom is Sarah), foster kids, and numerous grandchildren.

I loved hearing about my dear friend's life. It seemed as though I'd just left her home yesterday. "I always looked upon your mom as my big sister," I confessed to Sarah. "Losing touch made me so sad."

"Yeah, Mom says it was her fault because she didn't answer your last few letters." Sarah and I exchanged phone numbers, addresses, and e-mail instructions. It was already after nine in my time zone, so I assured her I'd be calling her parents the next day to catch up in person.

Then Sarah dropped her bombshell. "There's one more thing." She hesitated. "Your son wants to talk to you."

My dream collided with reality. My heart seized.

"But, Donna, only if it's not a problem for you or your family."

In my mind's eye, dozens of images whirled—dark hair, pink cheeks—a little boy—my angel from so long ago....

I sat rooted to my seat, yet a hummingbird's feather could have knocked me off the stool. I couldn't speak, find even one drop of saliva to swallow, or air enough to breathe. From deep inside I trembled. Tears blinded me, and I gasped, "Oh, Sarah, of *course* I want to talk to him."

From then on, I caught only snatches of Sarah's rushing monologue. She began to tell me about Joel. The first time I heard her say "Joel," his name felt familiar. Somehow, I *knew* it, although had anyone asked me before that minute, I couldn't have uttered it. I hadn't chosen a name; I wouldn't allow myself that most intimate gesture. In the crevices of my core being, along with the love I felt for my baby, I also knew his name was Joel.

"He's very sweet and loving and lots of fun, Donna. He's handsome too. He's great at soccer and baseball. He's totally awesome."

I heard her laughter and an almost reverent joy as she rushed on. "Oh gosh, Donna, you're gonna just *love* him! I can't wait for you to talk to him!"

Sarah told me Joel and his wife lived in Washington state. I peppered her with rapid-fire questions. She answered without hesitation. Her voice came animated, high-pitched. I grabbed a message pad and wrote J-o-e-l. I added a telephone number, an address.

Then it struck me. As though I received a blow to the face, the world shuddered to a solid silence. Sarah wasn't reciting just facts—she had real-time knowledge of Joel.

"Sarah, how do you know my son?"

Once again, she laughed. "He's my *cousin!*"

The couple I'd thought were Pam and Maurie's friends turned out to be Pam's brother, Bill, and his wife, Joan. Of all the potential parents out there, *they* were the ones who'd adopted my son.

God had revealed another bit of His glorious plan for me.

In spite of my joy, I was a physical wreck, trembling hard, breathing fast, dizzy with excitement. I knew without a shred of doubt I wanted to talk to my son—to hear him, learn about him, get a sense of him—but I told Sarah I couldn't do it that night. I was too terrified.

Through my tears, I stammered, "Sarah, I have to wrap my heart around this first. I'll call him tomorrow night at seven."

Chapter Nineteen

I knew I had two phone calls to make, and after I calmed myself a few minutes, I made the first one to Pam. I no longer worried about the time difference between Texas and Buffalo, New York—I was too excited. Sarah had obviously told her mother she'd found me. Pam answered my call on the first ring. Hearing her soft voice made me want to shout with glee.

We laughed and cried at the sound of each other as we fell back through time together. I heard Maurie's hearty laughter joining in from somewhere near Pam.

"Pam, how could you have kept this from me?"

"It was the hardest thing in the world, Donna. You *know* I couldn't tell you anything. I was desperate to tell you how much Joan and Bill would love him. But, most of all, I wanted you to know I'd always be there to watch over him too."

She chortled in her deep voice. "Joel is such a delight to his parents. He and his brother, Ross, played with our kids all the time. When he was a little boy, he knew about being adopted and that you'd lived with us. He'd ask me, 'Aunt Pam—tell me about my mommy.' I'd tell him he looked like you, he had your sense of humor, and I knew you would love him to bits if you could see him that day. He always wanted to know more, but I couldn't give him details. Later, I couldn't even give him your address."

Even stricter standards bound Maurie to silence. Pam said when Joel asked his uncle Maurie for information, he'd say, "I can't tell you anything. I'm sorry, Joel, but I'm her doctor."

Maurie came to the phone to say hello. The world turned taffy-sweet as I heard him tell me of the young man Joel has become.

"By the time Joel turned eighteen, I'd retired. My partner had all our office records. I called my attorney to see what I might be able to tell Joel. He advised me I couldn't access your hospital employment records—even the delivery records without your consent. Since we didn't know where you were, it kind of ended for us being able to help him."

Pam told me Joel had gone into the navy right after high school. A deep rift between Joel's dad and his aunt Pam had separated their families for years, but Joel had kept in touch with his aunt, his uncle, and his cousins. Despite him living in Washington and her in New York, he and Sarah now seemed especially close.

Pam and I ended our conversation anticipating my phone call to Joel the following evening.

• • •

When Jonathan and Stephanie were in high school, we taught swimming lessons in our backyard pool. I stood in the pool twelve hours a day. The water was a constant 84 degrees, but standing in it that long brought on hypothermia. It may have been ninety degrees outside, but at the end of the day when I came inside, I wrapped myself in layers of flannel. I shook violently for hours.

That June night when I made my next phone call to Wayne, my teeth chattered, and my body trembled with the intensity of those swimming lesson nights.

I was home alone when Sarah called. Working three hundred miles away, south of Houston, Wayne wasn't due to return for another two days. When I reached him on his cell phone, he happened to be on busy I-45, on his way to spend the night in the apartment we sometimes shared with Stephanie.

Before he could even finish his, "Hi, honey," I blurted out, "You'll never guess what! My son found me. Wayne, he *found me*! His cousin

Sarah just called me from New York, and she's Pam and Maurie's daughter, and Pam never told me, and ..."

Poor Wayne.

He kept saying, "Wait a minute. Wait a minute. I'm gonna run into someone—let me pull over here."

I'm sure the excitement of my jumbled newscast made it hard to grasp anything in the midst of my crying and laughing. Somehow though, in spite of the garbled delivery, the gist of it came through.

When he could focus on the cell phone, he said, "I can't believe it! This is fantastic. Honey, I'm shaking head to toe. Every hair on my neck is standing straight up, and I've got goose bumps all over."

I tried to fill him in on the details of what had transpired, starting back at the beginning of Sarah's call.

His joy overflowed as genuine as mine. Neither of us held any trepidation about speaking with my son. By now, we were both laughing. Then my husband's voice cracked, I heard him draw a long breath, and he began to sob.

"Donna, this is so amazing. For four months, I've been praying for a way to tell you we should look for your son. I know you've never looked, but I just kept feeling I needed to tell you we should start searching. And now, this happened..."

Jabez visions scampered through my mind. I'd begun praying his prayer exactly four months ago.

Wayne interrupted my musing as he asked, "Honey, when are you going to call him?"

Very much aware of my still-racing heart, I answered, "Tomorrow night at seven—if I live that long."

"Honey, did I tell you his name is Joel—Joel Martin Johnstone? Gosh, I wish you were here." I knew he had a full schedule of clients booked for the next day, but he didn't hesitate for a second.

"Yes, you told me his name. I'll move heaven and earth to get back up there to be with you when you make that call."

Wayne has always been and still is a hard worker. Three weeks a month, he headed south from our home, making a five-hour drive to his public accounting firm in Alvin. He left before sun-up on Monday, put in four twelve-hour days, and made it back to the lake somewhere around ten or eleven Thursday nights.

"You don't need to be alone for this. I'll cancel all my appointments tomorrow morning and head home." His voice came out in a croak. "Don't worry, honey, I'll be there."

When we finished talking, I still trembled with excitement as my mind retraced the past half hour.

I couldn't sit in my recliner, much less focus on a book or our most riveting DVD. I began to cry. Tears formed a steady stream and ran down my face. I blew my nose into dozens of tissues as I paced between the living room and office. I attempted to play the piano, but between wiping my tears away and blowing my nose, I found even music couldn't settle my mind.

Spent, I forced myself into bed somewhere around two in the morning. I didn't sleep, or even doze. I tossed and turned as the minutes crawled by. My past had caught up to me. I could no longer outrun it or silence its voices.

I willed the hours to pass between three a.m. and the most significant phone call of my life.

I knew no one else could make this call. Even with Wayne beside me, I alone would be responsible for the phone call. I would somehow have to convey the extent of the joy and hope with which I'd found myself blessed. Through the skinny windows along the side of my bedroom, I watched a thousand tiny stars beyond the pine trees. "The heavens declare the glory of God; and the firmament showeth His handiwork." (Psalm 19:1)

In the darkness, I cried as I thanked God for this son named Joel. "Thank you, Lord, for your grace, and for letting me know my son is alive and well. Thank you for answering me with the blessings you promised."

Thousands of times over the years, I'd wondered if my son was angry with me. Could he forgive me? Would he forgive me? Questions beyond the ones I'd already asked myself surfaced like debris in a flood. What if one phone conversation was all Joel wanted? What if I never saw him in person? What if his parents forced him to choose a limited relationship with us? What if my children did?

My faith had grown enough that I knew God would supply the right words if I asked. I spent the remainder of the night praying for guidance. I made a frantic entreaty, "Dear God, please help me find the right words tomorrow. Give me courage to ask his forgiveness for handing him over to strangers. Oh, God, you know I did what I thought was best for him, but has he hated me all these years? Do I need to prepare my heart for his anger? Will you lend me strength?" During the night, God guided me as I made my plan.

Tomorrow I'll speak to my firstborn son. Jonathan doesn't even know he has a brother. Help me find the right way to tell him about Joel. Then I'll call Stephanie.

Taxed and worn, my heart continued beating that morning as the eastern sky blushed from rose to pink to apricot. I made my first cup of coffee. As my mind filled with Joel in waves of excitement, curiosity, nervousness, and dread, my heart crashed about in my chest.

Tail aloft, my constant companion, our yellow Lab, Danny, trotted ahead of me as I, still in my pajamas, carried an orange cappuccino across the deck to the swing. The colors strewn across the sky now tinted the lake below. I couldn't help reveling in the moment. Danny settled at my feet, and I eased my bare toes into the soft blond fur along his back.

In a sense, I enjoyed being alone with my thoughts. Apart from Wayne, I wasn't ready to share this magnificent drama with anyone. I filled my morning with menial housekeeping chores—anything to keep the clocks progressing toward seven p.m. At my desk, I read business e-mails and then opened my personal account. The first message was from Pam. After our talk, she'd spoken to Joel on a three-way conversation with Sarah. I read her short e-mail a few times but couldn't find anything between the lines.

It bothered me that I had no idea of Joel's reaction to Sarah's news of finding me. A troubling thought scurried out of a dark corner of my mind. From Sarah's description, Joel had an easygoing personality and seemed well liked by everyone. What if he was an angry person on the inside? What if he felt abandoned? Maybe his life wasn't as it seemed to others.

I vowed I'd catch Pam up after I'd talked with Joel. She ended her e-mail by saying she felt overwhelmed.

Overwhelmed? Ha! You have no idea what overwhelming is, Pam!

Wondering and worrying about what could be in store for me led me through the next couple of hours. About lunchtime, I checked for new e-mails and received another extraordinary shock.

> Hi Donna,
>
> I'm Joel's wife, Shelley. I can't even begin to tell you how excited we both are to have finally located you. We've thought of you countless times over the years and wondered if we'd ever get to know you.
>
> Joel's cousin Sarah has been dogged in her search for you. I doubt if we'll ever be able to thank her and Aunt Pam adequately for their efforts.
>
> I look forward to thanking you in person for choosing to give birth to Joel. He is a most amazing man, easy to love, and full of life. He makes my world beautiful and I can't wait to share him with you.
>
> Best wishes,
> Shelley

> Shelley,
>
> *You* made my day with "easy to love and full of life." I *cannot* wait for tonight. I'm planning on calling at 7:00 p.m. my time. I'm already choking up; I don't know how

this will go, but it will be an awesome experience for all of us.

You're so sweet to think of sending me a note—I too can't wait to get a glimpse of your lives.

Hugs,

Donna

Shelley and I e-mailed a couple of more times during the day. She asked if it was true that I'd lived in Washington state for a little while.

No, honey, I've not even travelled to Washington. Yet.

Shelley wrote of their daughter Mandy, whose guardianship they'd established at age thirteen after she came to them for foster care. "Mandy and Joel formed a very special bond, and Joel developed an extraordinary adeptness at handling some of the rougher teenage patches."

Shelley let me know Joel left earlier that morning to work out of town. He planned to call me from his hotel once he settled into his room. She stayed in touch with him during the day as he drove, filling him in on the details of our e-mails. "We, too, are having lots of trouble concentrating. Joel had a sleepless night pondering the recent happenings. He was a roller coaster of emotions."

By the time of our fifth exchange, I no longer attempted house or office work. I was too excited. I e-mailed a photo of Jonathan and Stephanie. Shelley said Joel snail-mailed pictures to me before he left that morning.

She said Joel should call around five.

Five? Wayne won't get here until seven. Recalling how he'd almost wrecked on I-45 when I gave him startling news, I didn't dare call him and ask him to drive faster.

The final hours dragged by as I hovered near the phone.

Chapter Twenty

Back in the good ol' days—for me, the fifties and sixties—rolls of cotton came in a dark blue box. When the phone rang a little before five, some gremlin had wrapped an entire roll of cotton around my tongue. I grabbed the phone and somehow managed a saliva-less, "Hello?"

The sweetest sound I've ever heard came through the receiver.

"Hi, Mom. It's Joel."

I couldn't stem the tide of my emotions any longer. In less than a second it became obvious Joel couldn't either. Although occasional periods of silence punctuated our sighs, we spent the next hour crying, laughing, and talking ninety-to-nothing.

That glorious June night, my son and I began rebuilding a conduit of love as old as time—a bridge spun from the pure gold reserved for a mother and her child. With amazing ease, our bridge spanned the miles between northwestern Washington and the piney woods of east Texas.

Joel said he'd searched for me for more than twenty years throughout Washington state. Years earlier, his aunt Pam told him I'd lived at their home, that my first name was Donna, and that I'd married someone named White. She and Maurie weren't sure where I lived but suggested it might have been Washington. It seems she confused the DC honeymoon trip Don and I took twenty years earlier with Washington state.

"Mom, I spoke to fifty-eight Donna Whites in the state of Washington. Not one of them knew anyone by the name of Pam

Dewey. Aunt Pam also told me she thought you'd graduated from Lake George High School."

I told Joel I'd only gone there for part of ninth grade and graduated from Glens Falls High. He laughed. "I argued for a long time with that poor school secretary, telling her you would be on their records. She argued right back, and said, 'No, she isn't!'"

Dead end after dead end ensued until his cousin Sarah told Joel he'd looked for me by himself long enough. She volunteered her computer skills and marshaled unwavering resourcefulness to find his birth mother.

• • •

I prayed for years for my son to be in good health and always to feel his adoptive parents' love. I also allowed myself the luxury of less important things, wondering what he looked like. Sarah told me Joel was handsome. Listening to him talk and laugh, I tried to decide who he sounded like.

Now, for the first time since I heard his lusty cry in the delivery room, I heard him crying again. I could tell he tried to choke it back. I attempted to speak without my voice breaking, too, and we traded more lulls in our conversation.

When he could speak, Joel's deep voice came across the miles warm and soft. Polite and self-assured, he asked gentle questions and laughed easily. He sounded so much like my dad!

Where did he grow up? What were his parents like?

I learned of his family's lakeside home, built by his grandfather in a small community north of Rochester.

"I have great parents, and I've had a good life. I have an older brother who's also adopted. My parents are always there for us. My mom is still my biggest fan when I play soccer or baseball. She never missed any of my games when I was a kid."

"What did you do after you got out of school, Joel?"

"I joined the navy right after high school and became a Seabee. I loved welding and got special training in utility work." He chuckled. "I'd be a Seal if there weren't any sharks in the ocean!

"When I was stationed in California, I met Shelley. She was in the navy too. The first time I saw her, she looked so beautiful I stared at her all evening. We were married in 1986, and the navy sent us to Adak, Alaska, for a couple of years.

"When we got out of the navy, we decided to live in Washington. We both liked the Northwest." Pausing a few seconds, he added, "We hoped we might be able to find you."

He told me he was still a navy reservist and worked for a gas utility company.

Reaffirming one another, reciprocal questions and answers flowed between us. We covered a multitude of topics, from a shared love of swimming to reading and the outdoors.

Finding that we both had a passion for Labrador retrievers, Joel chuckled as I described my sweet Danny, intent on catching a bug as it crawled along the floor at my feet. Like a big man on campus, Danny strutted, circling his prey, brows furrowed, eyes glued to the target, ears pricked, and tail wagging. Every inch of him quivered as he anticipated some action. He waited until the last possible second before pouncing. All ninety pounds of him landed on a small spider scuttling for refuge under the edge of a rug.

In turn, Joel told of flying home from Alaska, Shelley cuddling next to him, their black Lab, Cain, riding in a crate in the baggage area. The plane was a commercial airliner filled with military personnel. He described squirming in his seat while listening to incessant, plaintive barks from behind the flimsy wall separating the passenger area from baggage and small cargo.

As the long barrage continued to grow louder and more insistent, the crew became very worried about this poor dog. Joel sheepishly confessed Cain was his when the flight attendant demanded the dog's owner identify himself.

Cain looked very satisfied and quieted as his master joined him in baggage for the rest of the trip. Joel said he couldn't blame the dog—he didn't much enjoy huddling in a parka and riding in the unheated cargo area either.

Joel and I compared books we'd read and found we had a number of mutual favorites. His voracious reading habit corresponded with that of his maternal grandmother, his siblings…and mine.

It took me a long time before I could bring up my ultimate torment. Regardless of the circumstances of his family and upbringing, could he ever accept my act of placing him for adoption as one of love rather than desperation? When I could bear it no longer, I finally asked, "Joel, can you ever forgive me?"

His hesitancy in answering gave me the sense it was as difficult for him to reply as it was for me to ask. I dreaded what he might say and braced myself against the edge of the counter.

"Mom, there's nothing to forgive! I'm just glad Sarah found you. I've looked for you since I was a little boy."

Joel's voice dropped to an even deeper pitch, and I had to strain to hear him.

"I used to follow ladies in the mall. When I found one who looked like me I'd think, 'She looks like me. I wonder if she's my mother.' I wasn't unhappy; it's just something I always wanted—to know *who* I was, and what you looked like. I used to tell myself that's all I needed—to see you just one time—even from across a room somewhere."

He paused again. "But, Mom, as soon as I heard you say 'hello,' I knew I had to know everything about you!"

Putting small talk aside, I assured Joel he could take the rest of my life to ask me anything he wished. He began by asking about my work, and I told him of my nursing and business careers.

He asked me to tell him more about my family, beyond what Shelley had told him on his cell phone as he traveled.

"So, I have a brother and a sister, right?"

"Yes, Jonathan's thirty-four. He's quiet until you get to know him, but he has a quick mind and a dry wit. He's very smart, and just like his dad, he seems to have a photographic memory. Jonathan is tall and has—well, he used to have—blond, curly hair. He keeps it so short now it's hard to say what it looks like. He loved camping and scouting, and earned his Eagle Scout from the same troop his dad did. He's played soccer most of his life."

"Me too, Mom! Does he still play?"

"He's not in a league now, but he plays occasionally. He joined the marine corps reserves when he was a sophomore in college. He finished a stint in Kuwait and Iraq last fall. He scheduled fuel transport from Kuwait up to Baghdad airport and sometimes drove the tankers himself. Even though I tried to be brave about it, I was a mess inside until he got home."

Joel was called to active duty about a month after 9/11 and went to Thailand, where he did training exercises with both US and Thai Navy Seals. "Mom was a train wreck until I got home too."

We spoke of both my sons' reservist experiences—how difficult it was to be away from family, knowing how much they were missing at home, trying to show bravery for those of us left behind.

My breath still came in quivers. We'd been talking a long time, and yet I remained glued in position on the edge of my stool. The uniqueness of the evening struck me. Never in my wildest dreams did I think I'd learn anything about my child. *My son* was speaking about his youth, his parents, and his life.

I never wanted the call to end.

CHAPTER TWENTY-ONE

When I mentioned Jonathan's love of golf, I found I had two sons who loved to play. I pictured them laughing, walking down a fairway together with another avid golfer, their uncle Dale. I told Joel about my oldest brother, his wife, Pam, and his five children.

I hurried on to tell him about his sister. "Stephanie's thirty-one, and she's a nurse. She works at the University of Texas Medical Branch in Galveston in the surgical intensive care unit. Most of her nursing is focused on neurosurgical patients."

As is usual for me, I blurted out my hopes in the form of assumptions. "Joel, you're going to love her! She's pretty and lots of fun. She's working on her fourth degree—this one's in interior design. She has an artistic flair, and she's very stylish." I couldn't help laughing as I told him her best friend called her "Prissy Missy."

Swallowing hard again to keep steady, I went on. "Stephanie gave us a terrible scare last year. She had a malignant melanoma on the back of her arm. Even though she had the spot less than a week, her surgeon removed fourteen lymph glands. The cancer had already invaded four of them. She needed a skin graft from her hip to fill in the hole that was left."

There was also a hole in our bluest sky of conversation. I could hear Joel breathing, but it took a few more seconds before he replied.

"Whoa! But... I mean, she's okay now—right, Mom?"

"She's okay, honey. Melanoma is a nasty cancer. It can return any time, so for the rest of her life, she'll need CAT scans to check for recurrences in her brain or lungs, but she's fine now."

Neither of us spoke for a few minutes. In the silence, I reflected on my sweet Stephanie, her gentleness and loving nature. I hated the deep-dimpled scarring left on the back of her arm—it *looked* like a nasty cancer. I couldn't bear the thought of her dealing with this cancer ever again.

I waited for Joel to ask another question.

"What about my grandparents?"

· · ·

My father, the man who called me "my little chickadee" all of my life, died of a massive heart attack in 1990. Dad and Marianne ended up with ten children—three of his, three of hers, and four of their own. He instilled a love of music, the outdoors, and animals in each of us. As I grew older, I came to understand his foibles as not unlike my own. I speak the truth of my father as I understand it, and I will always love and miss him.

He and my mother shared a past love, a long marriage, and three children. Most important, Mom put aside her initial feelings toward him after their divorce, and the two of them remained friends until he died. Their friendship not only helped me adjust to a life in which my father absented himself part of the time but influenced my post-divorce relationship with Don.

I told Joel my parents divorced, but I remained close to both of them until they died. I filled him in on my father's life, and told him most of my family still lived in upstate New York, around Glens Falls and Lake George. "Joel, your grandfather is gone now, too, but with nine children left, you have plenty of aunts and uncles. I hope you get to meet all of them! My brother Dave lived the closest to me, in Arkansas. He died of lung cancer a couple of years ago. He smoked a long time, and it finally caught up with him.

"My mother was a very special woman who loved antiques and gardening, but loved children even more. When I was in high school, she worked as a nanny and ended up traveling all over the country. Your Gran came to Pam and Maurie's when you were about six weeks old, and she was the only one in the family who knew about you. Oh, Joel, she would've been so thrilled to know you."

I prattled on, telling Joel how his grandmother had spent every winter with me since I'd moved to Texas in 1967.

"Wayne put up with her spending winters here and had no problem with her moving in with us when she was eighty-four. He was always a good sport about being a target for the zingers she could deliver in a nanosecond."

The vision of me conversing with my son had resided in my daydreams for years, and always in these dreams I saw my mother sitting nearby, watching, laughing, and putting in her own nickel's worth. Although the distinctive sound of her laughter had faded since her death, I heard it now mix with Joel's deep chuckling. It made this wonderful instant bittersweet as I related a few anecdotes about his Gran, loving his laughter as I spoke. He quieted as I described the hole her death left in our family.

"Your grandmother and I had a long, long time to say how much we loved one another before we said good-bye. She was ninety-three when she died, and we all miss her. I still think about her every day."

I twisted on my stool to look out the windows toward the lake. The sky cast a glow of golden colors by now. I could see the lake calm and quiet, and I could hear the whisper of the pines near the house. As I spoke to Joel, I wished for him to be near me, to share the serenity of life on the water's edge.

Glancing up at the clock and seeing it was nearly seven, I realized Wayne should arrive home soon. He still didn't have any idea that Joel called as soon as he'd reached his hotel. I wished he'd arrived in time for at least part of this incredible phone call.

"I've been married to Wayne for twenty-two years. He's been a wonderful, loving husband, and a good second dad to Jonathan and Stephanie. His son and daughter both live in Texas, and he has three grandchildren.

"His accounting practice is near Houston, but some weeks he can arrange his schedule to consult from here. We feel very fortunate when we work in my office next to each other all day."

The time Joel and I spent moved too rapidly for me to share all I felt about my husband, how proud I felt of his professionalism and work. I didn't tell him how happy it made me when he referred to our home as a peaceful refuge.

I didn't say that my marriage to Wayne felt as comfortable and fun as a middle of the night come-as-you-are party. No matter how you were dressed for the party, your best friends didn't mind your favorite raggedy nightgown. They stood in theirs, laughing with you.

I hoped to know Joel well enough in the future to express how I loved that Wayne still kissed me on the neck, how he reached for my hand in the night.

Joel and I had talked for more than an hour, and by now, both our voices sounded husky. The brief glimpses of his life seemed difficult to assimilate in one evening—still I had to know more.

From the way he talked, the special lure of knowledge about me caused him to thirst for a greater depth and intimacy as well. I hoped for additional time later to tell him more about my family. I didn't feel it my place to suggest another contact from him, so I waited for Joel's lead.

"Wayne sounds like a great guy! I'm glad you're happy."

• • •

I'd always dreaded the questions he might ask about his father. The moment I learned I could talk to my son, I resolved not to answer those questions on the telephone. Joel's question came toward the end of the conversation.

"Tell me about my dad and what happened, Mom."

I take full responsibility for my own actions the night I conceived my firstborn. I'd played a role in the date rape by the way I handled myself. In defense of my drinking and his father's behavior, we were both young and immature. Nevertheless, that which caused me to be wary enough to end our engagement remained undeniable.

Part of my management skills involved an irrevocable conviction—that I would always be just. I strived for my daily actions to resound with fairness. I found now, however, "fairness" was fantasy—an elusive essence I was both unable and unwilling to capture. I would give Joel the statistics of his father, the photos I'd kept, and tell him of the good times, but the rest would remain where it belonged, sealed in my distant past.

"I will, Joel, but that's a face-to-face conversation."

He answered without hesitation. "That's fine—I was just curious. It's funny though…" And for a time, he paused. "I've never had a desire to know my father, and I never knew why. But I knew I had to find you somehow."

I heard him take a deep, quick breath.

"You know I want to come and meet you, Mom, right?"

Giddy with relief, I said, "Of course you have to come see me!"

"That's good, because we already have reservations—we're coming July the second!"

After all the years of pain, my shame began to dissolve in God's grace. I looked up at the ceiling, but fresh tears came in spite of my pitiful attempt to stop them.

We ended our conversation with a promise to talk again the next night. Although my heart tap-danced at triple speed and my mind still raced in circles, my limbs felt rubbery. I remained at the kitchen counter for several minutes before I dared get off the stool.

I knew Wayne would want to hear every detail of Joel's conversation, so I decided to await his arrival rather than call his cell phone and divert his attention. He'd almost driven into another car the last time I distracted him…

I poured myself a glass of water, picked up my cell phone, and speed-dialed Jonathan's number.

After a brief hello, he asked, "What's up, Mom?"

"Honey, I've got some *big news.*"

"What, you got another Lab?"

"No—it's much bigger news than that."

"You bought more lake property?"

"No, honey, I didn't."

I couldn't restrain myself another second. "Jonathan, you've got a big brother."

I held my breath as I waited for his mind to catch up. I was used to Jonathan's quick retorts. This one took several seconds.

"Yeah, right. So, what else is new?"

I assured him I wasn't joking. Several times.

When I finished telling him about Joel, he sounded more hurt than I imagined he might, and he asked, "Why didn't you ever tell me? Didn't you think I could handle it, or what?"

"I never told you because I didn't think it would ever affect your life, Jonathan. When I gave him up for adoption, I never expected to know anything more about him. They sealed adoption information in those days. I didn't know who my baby went to, and they didn't know me."

I tried to reassure him I'd told very few people about Joel. I confessed Joel's adoption remained part of my past because it hurt me to speak of my guilt, worry, and fears. I also revealed my inner belief that if people knew I'd had a baby, even after all this time, they'd look upon me as an immoral woman with little character. Worst of all was my fear *Jonathan* might look at me that way.

"You were a nurse, Mom. How'd you ever let yourself get pregnant?"

His brutal frankness hit me hard. I could've told him I didn't have any experience yet, that we hadn't discussed birth control at home or in nursing school, and I'd have been very honest. It wasn't easy to discuss any of this with my son, but I owed him long-hidden truths. I felt my face grow flame-hot as I relived the feelings of all the embarrassment I'd experienced for so many years.

He stayed quiet when I shared the details of what happened to me all those years ago.

"Today it would be called a date rape, but in the sixties a rape was considered a girl's own fault, especially if she knew the man and had been drinking. I had been. In fact, I'd been purposeful about getting numb with Scotch.

"For months, I had some uneasy feelings about a number of incredible tales spun by the person I thought I'd marry. When one story proved false beyond any doubt, I decided to end our relationship. I couldn't imagine life with someone who didn't seem capable of distinguishing fact from fiction.

"I told him I thought it would be best if we didn't see each other any more. I could see how confused he was, and when I looked up, I saw the depth of his pain. I stumbled and crawled upstairs, drunk and miserable."

I had trouble getting out the rest of the story—it was so hard to tell this to my own son. I took a deep breath to stall for a few more seconds. "An hour later, my drinking led to my inability to fend off a frustrated, angry young man. No matter how I struggled and pleaded, I couldn't deter him.

"Jonathan, I was horrified that someone who professed to love me could commit such an unspeakable act. When the front door slammed downstairs, I got into the shower and turned on the cold water."

Jonathan remained silent when I told him Joel's father left after he attacked me, and I'd never heard anything more from him. The memory of the shower came in strong waves. Instead of reliving the feel of icy water though, I felt as though someone poured scalding water over me. Tense moments ticked by while I tried to find the next words.

"His actions reinforced the decision I'd made weeks before, and by morning, I was even more resolute. I swore he'd never be a part of my life again.

"Weeks later, I realized I must be pregnant. Every time I thought about the physical aspect of that night, I was ashamed. I felt it had been my fault. At the same time, I felt betrayed."

For a long time I hated the young man who had let me down in the cruelest of all ways, but once I felt my belly fill, a basic emptiness replaced the hate. I suppose he felt a terrible bitterness toward me as well, because he never called me again. I was lonely, but I didn't miss him in my life—I never had another desire to speak with him—and with all my soul, I felt he didn't deserve to know. To my knowledge, he had no idea of what began at our ending.

"Jonathan, things were so different then. It was a terrible disgrace for me to be pregnant and not married, but I never considered an abortion for a minute. I couldn't bring my shame upon our family, so I didn't tell anyone at home, not your grandfather, your uncle Dale, not even Gran. I felt I couldn't raise a child by myself. It took months to reach that conclusion, but I put him up for adoption."

I didn't tell Jonathan that no matter the circumstance of conception, if I faced the future alone given the mores of the sixties, I'd make the same decision for Joel's sake. It wasn't the time to reveal that I didn't yet know how strong a mother's survival instinct is. Looking back, I felt that I probably could have raised a child by myself.

Most of all I couldn't tell Jonathan how giving away my own baby had shredded my heart, for fear of how long I'd cry on the phone. None of us likes to hear our mothers cry. Or our fathers.

· · ·

Dad and I stood together beside the casket, looking at Grandma Granger. Dressed in a dress she often wore to church, thin hair puffed around her sleeping white face. Tears ran down my cheeks as I willed Grandma's chest to move beneath the black fabric.

The stillness of the dim room suffocated us.

My father's sudden, strangled gasp frightened me. As I jerked toward him, he crushed me against his chest and burst into tears. I'd never seen my father cry.

I saw my father now as a man. Strong, hard working, invincible. Vulnerable.

The few seconds we clung to each other sharing our sorrow didn't last long, but it changed my history, made my life more than just years, made me love him even more. That grief-filled moment glued itself to me.

. . .

I realized Jonathan was asking another question. "What did you say, honey?"

Big sigh.

I imagined him thinking, *Mom is acting normal—not paying attention again.*

"I said, 'So, what does Joel do?' Where does he live, Mom? Is he married?"

It was such a relief to be talking about Joel. I still didn't have a feeling for how Jonathan was taking all of this, but I desperately wanted to tell him about his brother. I plunged ahead, sharing what I'd learned about Joel's life. I described what I knew of Shelley, Joel's family in New York, and his work. At the end, I explained his Seabee reservist status.

Ever the marine, Jonathan belted out, "Navy! Did you say *navy?* I am *so* sorry!"

The tension snapped like a dried twig, and I laughed until tears ran down my cheeks. We spoke with ease afterward, and ended our talk with Jonathan asking if he could be the one to tell his dad about Joel. I felt Don would be happy for me and pleased to have our son relay the news.

CHAPTER TWENTY-ONE

Three years earlier, as Stephanie and I sat in Adirondack chairs on our townhouse patio, I told my daughter about my long-ago pregnancy. I'm not sure what triggered it, but I also revealed my baby's adoption and that only Gran, her dad, her "Uncle Ron," and Wayne knew of my past.

I should've known God prompted me to divulge this history to Stephanie. He prepared each of the people I loved, one heart at a time.

Like my mother, at first Stephanie expressed sadness at my being alone through the pregnancy. As my anguish of signing away the rights to ever know my baby sank in, her slender pale fingers reached across the arm of my chair. She understood the implication that she'd missed knowing her brother. Taking my hand, her blue eyes spilled tears through dark lashes. She whispered, "Do you ever think about him, Mom?"

I managed, "Almost every day for the past thirty-five years."

She held my hand a long time. My revelation obviously affected her, yet we seldom spoke of it again until I called her after talking to Jonathan.

Her excitement crackled like lightning through the phone when I told her I'd talked to Joel.

"Oh, Momma! That's wonderful! I'm so happy for you. Aren't you just dying to see him?"

"Yes, I am, honey. If I lived to be a hundred, I never thought this would happen. Imagine—you have a brand-new brother, and I'm *sixty* years old!"

As we cried, she repeated the same questions all the rest of us asked. She marveled at the sweetness of Shelley's e-mails. I could almost feel her anticipation at Joel and Shelley coming for a visit.

• • •

My mother, Stephanie, and I have always been close enough for Wayne to refer to us as "three peas in a pod." After she died, I'd placed Mom's ashes in a beautiful English biscuit jar from the Cayman Islands, feeling my mother would be pleased at her unique urn.

We no longer needed to be close to Mom's doctor. I needed to get out of the run-down house we rented, and the idea of living at the lake drew me to action. A friend helped me pack our belongings for the move to the lake. Not knowing its contents, she placed the biscuit jar in an unmarked box with contents from my living room. Along with almost one hundred other boxes, we unloaded the containers into any available space.

Adding an entire household, as well as the contents of my business office to our already furnished lake house presented a great challenge. Many boxes ended up stacked on our screened porch, along with the sixty-five boxes of antiques Dale sent me from Mother's house. As time and space allowed, I'd been sorting and storing the contents of these cartons for more than two years, but I'd not found the now infamous biscuit jar.

On the phone that evening, I reminded Stephanie how many one-sided conversations I'd found myself carrying on with my mother as I searched for the box that held her urn. We laughed through our tears at how delighted Gran would've been to witness the recent events about Joel.

"Stephanie, I can almost hear Gran when we meet in heaven, 'Oh, sure. You left me out on the porch for two years, and I didn't even get to hear about Joel.'"

How she would have loved him! I hated he didn't get to hear her stories, her funny retorts, that he could never witness her fortitude, or share her life lessons.

"Good night, sweet daughter, and little sister of *two* big brothers. I love you."

• • •

All the tears, adrenaline rushes, and jangling nerves dissipated. I felt like lettuce left in the veggie drawer too long—dried up, wilted, brittle around the edges.

Around six-thirty, Jonathan called me. "So, Mom, I know all of this must've been quite a shock. Are you doing okay?"

His concern, couched in a simple question, touched me. Jonathan had been my baby who cuddled and held tight to me as we rocked. As a toddler, he spent hours in various laps following along in his storybooks.

Stephanie, on the other hand, was always too busy to be held for long. Impatient, she squirmed and wriggled out of my arms to go to her big brother, rushing headlong after him like a puppy in hapless abandon.

When I took the children to the movies, Stephanie and I bawled through every sad part, but from age six, Jonathan turned his face aside in the dark theater and swiped away his tears. By the time he went to college, he was a quiet young man whose calls home were brief and infrequent. Our conversations revolved around surface issues, like sports and the national news. He still made me laugh when he called, and I knew he loved me, but I ached for him to express more of his feelings.

As events in the Middle East intensified, his reserve unit went to war. After their tour of duty while his unit shipped home, he volunteered to stay behind to complete the necessary paperwork, inventories, and turnover to the next motor transport group. He e-mailed me, *Those guys have wives and children waiting, Mom. They need to get back.*

In the fall of 2003, a much more family-oriented son returned from Iraq. From the day he left that hellish place, he began making regular calls home and speaking to us with genuine interest and spontaneity. His humorous observations made Wayne, Stephanie, and me laugh aloud. We loved having our fun-loving quipster home again.

In answer to his question about how I was faring, I assured him, "I'm rather overwhelmed with emotions, but I'm fine, honey. Thank you for asking."

Jonathan proved he got his sense of humor from both his parents when he relayed his dad's comment to the news about Joel. "Thank goodness. With all her Internet dating, I was worried your sister would end up dating her own brother one day!"

All fragments of concern about Jonathan's possible resentfulness of a new big brother were sucked into oblivion as he said, "I always knew I was a middle child. It explains so much about my life…"

• • •

I didn't have to wait long for the living room windows to glow with lights indicating a car in the driveway. Danny left my side to race through his doggy door. I could tell from his greetings that he'd met Wayne's familiar truck.

Still laughing at Jonathan's middle child remarks, I stepped into the illumination from the porch light. Already on the ramp from the driveway, an instant smile replaced my husband's worried expression and he stumbled into my arms.

Without even a hello in his ear, I launched in. "Honey, Joel's already called. He got to his hotel early. I didn't think it was him calling, and I answered the phone thinking it was you, and…"

"But, I wanted to be here for you. I didn't want you to be alone."

I nodded against his neck.

"And you're okay? Really?"

My whole body quivered in a sigh.

"It's okay, I'm here now." Wayne propelled me backward, murmuring, "I'm so relieved, Donna."

He turned me enough to walk to the sofa, then sank down and patted the cushion next to himself. "Now, take your time, but tell me everything."

• • •

On Monday morning, I opened my Texas bluebonnet-decorated mailbox and found a greeting card-sized envelope, addressed with unfamiliar handwriting. The return address area had a simple *Johnstone, Conway, Washington* scrawled in it. Joel's photographs had arrived from the other side of my new world.

I hurried down the driveway into the house and grabbed a counter stool. I shuddered with excitement as I extracted the first picture. Two smiling men and one woman stared back at me. Other men, seated along the same table, wore what appeared to be some sort of team t-shirt.

Imagine what it's like to start with a single distant glimpse of your baby and fast forward through a series of photos as your child grew into a man. Genetics play a part of our looks, but only God knows our children entirely from the inside out. He knows the number of hairs on their heads, loves and considers them always, but He doesn't FedEx photo albums.

I was stumped. Both men in this snapshot were pleasant-looking—one was exceptionally handsome. Could that one in the middle be Joel? He looked like my brother Dale. *The other guy seems too blond, but, then, Jonathan and Stephanie had both been blond at some point.* Neither now had my dark hair.

I flipped the photo over and read, "Taken after a softball game." No help.

The same handwriting graced the caption on the back of the next photo. "Shelley, her niece, and her mom."

The next photo confirmed not only which young man in the first picture was Joel but also that he was definitely *my* son. Beginning with his great-grandfather Roscoe, Granger men loved operating machinery. The bigger, the better, and the more dirt it moved, spread, or hauled, the more it was revered. My sister-in-law once said, "All Grangers are born with a steering wheel in their hands."

Here was Joel, operating a backhoe with "Jared, a neighborhood kid" sitting proud as a peacock on his lap.

The weeks sped by with long, nightly calls between Joel and me. I sat at my desk as we spoke—his photo propped in front of me, alongside those of Jonathan and Stephanie. Not one conversation passed the no-Kleenex-necessary test. Sighs and silences, and comfortable, aching, yet never-empty spaces punctuated our sentences.

We learned about each other's lives, siblings, and extended families. We talked about work, friends, and travels. We discovered additional mutual loves—mountains, sunsets, full moons. We discussed dozens more books. We chuckled at pet stories and adolescent adventures.

Joel laughed aloud at me telling him that although I'd "lost" my mother in her urn, I had many more boxes to address.

We talked of his childhood and visits to aunt and uncle's. Pam and Maurie had four boys, adopted two girls, and over the years, took in twenty-five foster children. "It was fun there because every time we went, Ross and I seemed to find we had a new cousin."

Joel was all boy. Although somewhat horrified, I couldn't help but laugh as he described dropping his cousin Leah down the laundry chute at Pam's—more than once. He maintained he'd received a good deal of encouragement from her brothers.

Because of the family issues and distance between his dad and aunt Pam, he hadn't seen his cousins for years. When Joel joined the navy, he kept in touch with Christmas cards and occasional phone calls.

During a call to invite Sarah to his parents' anniversary party, she said, "Joel, you've looked long enough for your mom. I'm going to help find her."

Through all our calls, Joel left no doubt of the deep love he felt for his mom and dad, his wife, and Mandy. By now, I fully understood Shelley's remark of his being "easy to love and full of life."

At times, we spoke as new friends, delighting in our discoveries. We revisited soccer and baseball games, drive-in dates, and first cars. We covered stupid pranks, courtships, and weddings.

As mother and son, we spent other precious moments confessing our haunted longings to see each other one day. To say those evening conversations were emotion-filled is like saying a Category-5 hurricane slamming into Miami is a wisp of wind skipping over empty dunes.

We marked off the pages of our calendars, detailing the descending countdown to July 2—the weekend of our new family's interdependence day meeting. As the golden sunsets of June's evenings spun into July, every week, every day, every minute validated our excitement. Before I slept, I prayed with a new vigor, "Please, Lord. Let this just be the beginning."

CHAPTER TWENTY-THREE

I imagined Joel and his family settling into their seats for the Seattle flight heading east. I'd sent him detailed directions for the three-hour drive from Dallas to our home. I cautioned him some cell phones don't get signals in our area.

From Shelley's e-mails, I knew they were all enthusiastic about coming, but I imagined Joel also had to be anxious about this somewhat frightening journey. Many of our conversations unveiled emotions about this day, and I felt he'd be traveling with myriad thoughts tumbling through his mind. I doubted he'd be able to concentrate on any single practical element of the trip.

My heart filled with understanding.

Months earlier, I'd agreed that friends could come to fish and swim over the Fourth of July weekend. Although they'd been to the lake several times, Wayne worried they'd be uncomfortable to find themselves caught in the middle of a major family event. He urged me to ask them to postpone their visit. "It just wouldn't be fair to Joel, or to them, honey. Call and tell them they can come up later."

I demurred, as they'd told me in several e-mails how they looked forward to being here and had scheduled a day off from work to come early. I also felt having guests here might be an icebreaker. I waited until our friends arrived late Thursday night before I revealed what was to happen the next evening.

Plain shock registered on their faces when I told them of having a child before I was married. I felt flushed as I talked, plowing on with the story. My narrative jumped and slipped from present to past and back again, as though I were hopping moss-covered rocks in a shallow streambed.

Every few minutes, Wayne interjected his own comments—obviously, he, too, was enthusiastic about the weekend. Near midnight, the four of us said good night and went to our bedrooms.

I heard their door shut at the other end of the house, and every now and then faint rumbles of conversation reached our room. I hoped it was too late for them to leave. I had plans to rely on their calmness over the next few hours.

After breakfast, we cleared the table as I spoke of Joel's search for me. The fact that Wayne and I both needed emotional support to make it through the day of waiting must have been evident, because our guests stayed.

Friday morning Wayne mowed grass and worked in the yard. Our guests fished off the shoreline. On the sun porch, I reviewed the weekend menus. Without all three of them keeping me focused and grounded, I don't think I could've made the wait without serious heart damage. We ate lunch and then dinner.

As the evening progressed, I paced, cried, and laughed at odd moments. I kept up an inane chatter, pausing long enough to race a hundred times to the driveway, after announcing I'd heard an approaching car. I felt, and certainly acted, manic.

Even with Shelley and Mandy for company, I guessed picking up baggage, getting a rental car, and navigating Dallas freeways filled with Friday night traffic would be a nightmare in slow motion for Joel. I thought the earliest I could expect them to arrive would be eight thirty p.m.

Nine o'clock came and went, as did nine thirty, then ten.

No sign of Joel.

No phone call.

There are very few streetlights in our rural subdivision. As the minutes dragged by, I became more and more unsettled at thoughts of Joel being lost, unable to get a cell phone signal. I asked again if the carport lights seemed bright enough to light the driveway. Finally, I'm sure for sheer self-preservation, Wayne drove out to the end of the subdivision to wait and guide Joel in for the last mile.

Not five minutes later, I saw headlights turning in the driveway and flew out the back door.

Even before the car came to a full stop, the driver's door opened. As I rounded the back of the car, I heard the gearshift clunk into park.

Arms reaching for me, my son climbed out, looked into my soul, and swept me into an embrace that washed us from an anxious sea to the solid rock of our forever. He whispered into my ear, "Hi, Mom. I love you."

• • •

As we all exhaled in unison, salty drops of joy ran down seven beaming faces. Our Labs, Danny and Vegas, joined the fray with general wriggling, thumping tails, and excited barks while we tumbled into the house amid hugs and handshakes.

We got the so-how-was-the-drive out of the way and toured the house. We brought in bags, exchanged gifts, and discussed sleeping arrangements. Despite trying to be polite and acknowledge conversations around us, Joel and I stole glances at each other a thousand times.

Oh, my, he's so handsome. None of the photos I'd seen did Joel's lean, tanned face, his expressive dark eyes, or his beautiful smile justice. I was so busy admiring his muscular physique, his straight posture, and his laugh bubbling from deep inside, I had yet to comprehend we shared genes, traits, and heritage.

Joel and I were the last ones to say good night. We embraced one more time before we went to our rooms to join our waiting spouses. I think everyone had difficulty sleeping that night.

• • •

We were up early the next morning to share the Johnstones' first look at the lake from the deck. I couldn't focus on anything but

Joel. If I wasn't hugging him, I was holding his arm, or sighing with Wayne over the blessings multiplying before us minute by minute.

Shelley's quiet natural beauty awed me, as well as her unselfish willingness to step back and let Joel and me have all the time we seemed to crave. Yet, in an instant, she'd be fully involved in a discussion. A well-spoken, delightful young woman, Shelley projected warmth to everyone.

Mandy seemed a bit shy at first, probably because the whole shebang overwhelmed her. Only at first. She turned out to be a terrific home version of *Saturday Night Live* and *Entertainment Tonight* rolled into one flamboyant eighteen-year-old.

Jonathan called to say he was sorry he wouldn't be able to make the ten-hour drive from west Texas to meet Joel.

Devastated he couldn't come because of work, I tried to be understanding.

Still, he wanted to be involved and asked, "What are y'all doin', Mom? Are you going anywhere today?"

"No, we're just hanging around and talking, waiting for Stephanie to get here."

Everyone had been company-polite and hadn't eaten much of a breakfast, but by noon we'd become relaxed and hungry. We gathered on the sun porch for lunch. For days, I'd tried to be an efficient hostess as I planned menus, shopped, and prepped food. I thought through the weekend's seating, grilling, and beer run arrangements. If my guests hadn't taken over many kitchen duties, I'm certain everyone would've been pounds lighter by Monday. They set out most of the main course while at times I flapped around in a state of total disarray. Shelley passed out plates and drink glasses as I heaped side dishes onto platters.

Stephanie arrived, red hair shining, eyes filled with bright sparkles, cheeks flushed pink with excitement. Grinning, she and Joel stared at one another and then embraced. Shelley joined in as the moment stretched into forever, and my heart burst.

Stephanie came behind the counter to give me an extra-long hug. She leaned close, whispering to me as everyone watched. I felt a little embarrassed—not wanting us to appear rude.

Squeezing my hand, she said, "Mom, I met 'the one.' I'll tell you more later." She slipped into the chair next to Joel.

Jonathan must have felt left out, because he called again. "What are y'all doing now? Did Steph get there yet? How's it going?" I knew he could hear everyone talking at the table in the background.

"Boy, Jonathan, you're going to be so sorry you didn't come. The food's great, the lake is calling us, and there's plenty of beer on ice!"

He came through the door, laughing, cell phone in hand. "Mom, I'm *very* sorry to be missing everything."

Wayne and I cried. For the one-hundredth time.

More handshakes, grins, hugs, and barks followed. Danny and Vegas were in their own kind of heaven, loving every minute of this people-who-love-dogs-filled weekend. We held hands, bowed our heads, and Wayne gave the most beautiful blessing I've ever heard. Everyone cried.

After lunch, we abandoned the house in favor of the lake, drifting down the path to the water in groups of twos and threes. The warm sunny day drew us to the lake's coolness.

We stood in chest-high water, talking and laughing as Vegas swam between Joel and Jonathan, begging for a splash of beer. Ninety-pound Danny thrashed back and forth noisily, hoping to entice me to the shore where he could stand. We women floated, sunned, and laughed as the guys told anecdotes. Every now and then, Shelley and Mandy wearied of standing and took turns having Joel hold them in his arms.

As the afternoon passed over my children and me, the others retreated to chaises and Adirondack chairs to doze or watch us from afar. I spent much of the time looking for similar mannerisms and gestures among my three offspring. Joel and Jonathan bantered about their service experiences and quickly formed the age-old alliance of brothers teasing sisters.

Stephanie swam away from them to where I stood, and told me about "the one." She'd met Kevin online a few weeks earlier. A former marine, he'd served as a police officer and was now a Houston firefighter. He also owned a window-treatment business.

After lengthy chats, Stephanie and Kevin met for dinner and began to date on a regular basis. Although she'd dated a number of men, she hadn't spoken to me about any serious relationships for several years. In the afternoon sunshine, she glowed as she talked about Kevin and his eight-year-old daughter, Kodi. I told her I'd not seen her so happy in a long time.

She tipped her head to the side, her hair fanned across the water, and she gave me a knowing smile. "That goes double for you, Mom."

That evening, some of us tanned and some sunburned, we lazed in chairs on the lawn, swapped stories, and watched the sun cast its last rose-amber spears across the water.

I was still exhilarated, but much to my embarrassment, I fell asleep in my recliner during a movie that evening. Wayne shook me awake and said everyone was going to bed. Silence suffused the house in just a few minutes.

I felt drained but filled to overflowing. The current day gone, tomorrow held the Lord's proclaimed day of rest. As I climbed into bed, I knew I would retain this night forever in my dreams.

In the morning, our friends left for home. After lunch, my three kids sat together and talked on an old church pew on the deck. Wayne and I watched from the swing as Joel held out his foot and said, "Look, Jonathan, we have the same feet." When Jonathan stretched his leg forward, Joel looked toward his sister and asked, "Stephanie, do you have our feet?"

"Oh no," she gasped, extending a polished and pedicured foot. "I have pretty feet!"

Later, much the same as I'd done with my mother in my youth, Joel and I swam together, gliding along the shoreline with an easy crawl stroke. Birds watched us as they circled high above the pines that stood along the banks like tall guardians. When we tired, we joined Wayne, Shelley, and the others in a loose circle in the cool water. We savored the newness of our bonds and relished their easy hold.

Early Sunday evening our next-door neighbor came over to pose us for our first official family photos. At dusk, we grabbed drinks and munchies, piled into the truck bed, and met friends Phil and Margaret at our pontoon boat in a nearby marina to watch a Fourth of July fireworks display. We oohed and aahed at the striking colors and patterns of the rockets against the night sky. Rockets burst in my heart.

But the fireworks weren't over yet for me this summer.

Chapter Twenty-Four

We ate breakfast the next morning with less excitement and noise than the day before. Knowing we'd be parting soon brought a subdued hush among us. No one seemed to want to be the first to signal the end of the visit by excusing themselves to pack. We lingered over cold coffee and muffin crumbs. It didn't seem possible or fair that the entire weekend had passed without my noticing the days disappearing.

I tried to be upbeat. *Nothing is over. It's just the beginning of our new family's life together.*

At last, everyone pushed back from the table and scattered to their rooms. Sounds of luggage whumping onto beds, an occasional shoe thudding to the floor, and the whine of closing suitcase zippers filled the house.

Jonathan faced the longest drive. I watched from the doorway as he shoved a duffle bag into the back seat of his car and made his way past me back inside for good-bye hugs. He embraced Wayne and then moved on down the waiting line.

He hugged Joel longer than I expected and took a step back.

"I'm glad you're my brother, Joel."

I sniffled into his shoulder through my bear hug.

Stephanie's parting produced equal emotion. She laughed and cried as she squeezed everyone. Still clinging to Joel, she gathered me in her free arm to bid me good-bye.

Joel and I moved outdoors and watched from the driveway as her red car rounded the bend in the road and disappeared out of sight.

Joel arranged baggage in the trunk of the rental car. Mandy and Shelley gave Wayne and me lingering hugs before they climbed inside. Joel clung to Wayne for a moment, shook his hand, and said he'd call after work the next day.

He swiveled toward me.

Parting so soon brought agony to us both. We couldn't speak.

Our time together ended that weekend as it had begun—with a long embrace and a mutual attempt to find a way to make the physical and emotional strength of the moment last as long as possible.

I've been alone in our home many times, but it's never seemed as quiet or empty as when Wayne and I went back inside that day. For a long time, we sat in stunned silence, each lost in private personal reveries.

I pored over the large photo album Shelley had brought. It made me feel such a part of their lives—reading the captions she'd written—seeing their home, vacation shots, and other family members in Florida and New York. I marveled at the number of friends she and Joel had made and kept close for the eighteen years of their marriage.

For dinner, Wayne and I raided our still-stuffed refrigerator. We ate leftovers and some of the dishes I'd prepared but somehow forgot to serve. We laughed as we realized we could eat appetizers, side dishes, and desserts for at least another week. Tired but happy, we went to bed early to revisit our dreams of the past three days.

The next morning I wrote to Shelley.

> July 6th, 8 a.m.
> Shelley,
>   Unequivocally you gave me the best weekend I've ever had. To know Joel was safe, healthy, and loved is all I've ever dreamed of learning. The gut-wrenching hugs, looking into his beautiful face, and hearing him say, "It's okay, Mom," has overloaded my heart forever. If I died today, no one who has seen me in the last 72 hours could ever think I didn't die a fulfilled woman.

Beyond your selfless sharing of Joel's attention, your warmth, *joie de vivre*, and shining spirit were such pleasures to experience. I regret I didn't get to know more *Shell*, but I can tell you are every woman's dream of a daughter.

Stephanie says she loves you both "to death," and Jonathan says he wouldn't have missed this for anything. Although he says I made all those stories up, he was pleased to be a part of finding a new brother and sharing Seabee/ Marine anecdotes. Wayne said a hundred times (compared to my millions), what a nice family we've found. We want to enfold you and be a part of your lives as often as possible.

I hope you got to sleep in a bit after your day of travel. I thought you looked so beautiful when I peeked in and saw you sleeping while you were here. The thrilling thing is that you're just as beautiful inside.

Love,
Mom

Shelley responded around noon.

Good morning! We made it home safely, and overall, the trip went well. Joel was quiet during most of our travel. Tears would roll down his cheek whenever he tried to share what was on his mind, so ultimately, he just didn't. I ache knowing I can't help him sort through all of these new feelings. However, you can, and I know you will.

I think there is a part of him that thought this would never happen. Then, to have it unfold with such a bounty of generosity and warmth, it was more than he ever dreamed.

You speak of the gift we've given you in knowing Joel. You can't even imagine the magnitude of the gift you have given *us*. That you and your family opened your home and hearts to us without a second thought is miraculous.

I'm so very thankful, too, that Jonathan and Stephanie were there to share in the weekend. I kept wondering what they must be feeling, thinking—they were so very gracious. You all were.

I need to get Joel back down there. I'd like to surprise him (maybe at Christmas) with a plane ticket to see you over his birthday. He should share his birthday with his birth mother, right?

There are many thoughts rambling through and over my brain this morning—things to thank you for, questions to ask. Please give a big hug to Wayne and a thank you for helping us feel so welcomed.

July 6th, 2:13 p.m.
TO: Stephanie
CC: Jonathan and Joel

I'm having a terrible time with loneliness, longing, and neediness today. I miss everyone so much.

I never could have imagined the beautiful things God planned for me.

All those years I thought and worried about my baby boy, whether he was safe and loved. It seems he has been all this time. I used to regret—not my giving him to someone else to love—but that I didn't nurse him a few days, hold him while I sang and rocked him, or even once, smell his baby scent.

In my head, I knew all those things would've made my decision impossible to carry forth, but my heart launched the thoughts anyway.

God was there through every one of those difficult months that stretched into years. It seemed forever before I was blessed to have my handsome Jonathan, and then you, my precious Stephanie. I don't love any of the three of you more, just each of you differently.

How I yearn to be with you all again! I know we'll have time together now, but I'm so afraid something will happen to us in the interim. I'm trying very hard to trust God will keep us safe. Still, it washes over me today that our next gathering can't happen soon enough.

Few mothers could be more proud of her children than I've been. Nothing could've made me happier than to see you together, and then hold, hug and kiss each of you.

To have Shelley here made it just superb. Didn't Joel pick the *best* sister-in-law ever? Mandy was the frosting on the brownies. We've made links that cannot be broken, no matter the span of time or distance.

Honey, I'll always appreciate that you and Jonathan made the effort to be here for this most special time.

Now you each know the way, and Wayne and I look for your footprints to make deep ruts to our back door. My heart is bursting with love, Mom

Joel called later that evening. He was working out of town again, and would leave on Saturday for a reserve weekend. He said he was ready to sell his house, quit his job and move to Texas to live next door to me. I assured him we would see each other often now, and he didn't need to move or leave a great job.

He wrote:

Mom,

That was a nice e-mail you sent Stephanie. Yes, you made me cry. Again! I'm beginning to feel dehydrated.

Shelley is supportive about my working out of town and being gone on weekends for reserve duty. She always has been—she is truly an amazing woman. I can hardly wait for all of you to get to know her better.

I just sent you a letter saying I didn't think I could wait until my Houston training school in October to see you again. I'm trying to schedule all of my upcoming work for the beginning of August.

Is it okay if I come back by myself in August to see you for a few days?

I love and miss you. Please take care of yourself. I love you. Joel

My screensavers morphed through beaming faces of my three children. I carried photos from our weekend in my purse. The pall of my shame had lifted at last, and I began to share our story with dozens of strangers.

I wrote to Pam and Maurie's daughter, Sarah to express my love and thanks for her role in helping Joel find me. I told her I thought of her as Joel's personal angel. It was difficult to find enough words to describe how much her assistance meant to all of us.

Joel and I continued our usual nighttime calls, supplemented by e-mails. He shared plans for the party he and his brother Ross were giving to celebrate their parents' fiftieth wedding anniversary in September. His pride at their marital milestone was evident, and he looked forward to seeing old friends from his youth in New York. Although Joel's dad and his aunt Pam hadn't been close for a number of years, he said he hoped she and Maurie would make the drive from Buffalo to the Rochester area for the party.

Joel also shared his struggle with the need to inform his parents of what had transpired since June, fearing he might cause them anxiety or pain. His mom had discouraged his searching for me when he was young, and he felt his news would be more difficult for her than for his dad. He didn't want to appear disloyal or selfish, yet he recognized he had to tell them the truth.

I could only be supportive and sympathetic. I encouraged him to unburden himself as soon as possible, as I assured him of all mothers' innate resilience.

In the end, he wrote his parents a letter, telling them his long search for his birth mother was over at last. He reassured them of his constant love, respect, and devotion. He asked them to be happy for him, as they knew how long he'd searched and how much it meant for him to meet his brother and sister.

As he described it, the letter sounded beautiful; how it might sound to Joan terrified me.

Chapter Twenty-Five

Months earlier, Wayne, Stephanie, and I had planned a late summer vacation in upstate New York. I was eager to see Dale and his family. Even though I'd left my hometown forty years earlier, he and I remained close.

When I'd moved to Buffalo, the thought of talking to Dale about my pregnancy made me feel more ashamed than telling my parents, so he knew nothing about Joel.

Now, as I packed the largest of our suitcases, I smiled, feeling as though I should be sending out birth announcements. I contemplated the sight of Dale's face when I told him he had a new nephew—one who was thirty-eight years old.

I called Pam and Maurie and told them our plans of visiting in Glens Falls. To my delight, they said they'd stop there on their way to Maine for vacation.

Stephanie e-mailed her July Fourth pictures to Joel. He described an enormous sense of closure in his thank you reply and joy because his wait had ended.

> It means a lot to me that you and Jonathan made the trip—it also shows how much you love our mom. I talked to her last night and I still can't help crying. I'm an emotional wreck. I can't concentrate on anything, and all I can do is think of each of you in Texas. If you'll have me as a brother, any time, anywhere, I'll be there for you.
>
> Have a great time in New York. I love you. Joel

• • •

As the plane banked in a gentle spiral, I looked out the window toward the Albany Airport. Farms, squashed-together houses, and parking lots seemed to rise up to meet us. Car windshields sparkled in the late afternoon sun as though studded with tiny gems.

Dale approached the baggage area, his handsome face wreathed in a broad smile. He spotted Stephanie and spun her around in his arms. He released her, clasped Wayne's hand, and then grabbed me. His embrace reminded me of my dad's—strong, brief, honest. His scent, almost imperceptible, was all Dale: subtle, musky, expensive.

My brother caught us up on his family's summer happenings and his newest teenage driver's exploits during the hour-long drive north. It was torture, but I waited until we arrived in Glens Falls and were in Dale and Pamela's kitchen before I launched into *our* summer. For a full minute, they listened in utter stillness, Pamela grinning from ear to ear. Everyone could see we'd caught my brother off guard. Like a series of masks, confusion, disbelief, and then pleasure slid over his countenance.

The news of Joel truly astounded him. "I can't believe it! I just can't believe I never knew a thing. I'm shocked!"

As usual, I cried as I related the phone calls and Joel's visit. I described Joel's resemblance to Dale both as a baby and now, and how he shared Dale's athletic gifts and love of golf. I told them of my vision of Jonathan, Joel, and Dale teeing off in the mists of a summer morning. Of course, I passed around my photos. Laughing over the photo of Joel operating a backhoe, they agreed he was definitely a Granger.

Dale's whole-hearted, unquestioning acceptance filled me with welcome relief—as much as I would feel if Dad was still alive and I'd just been able to tell him about Joel.

At noon the following day, the parking lot of the elegant old Queensbury Hotel echoed gales of laughter as Pam and Maurie

Dewey and I held each other close for the first time in thirty-eight years. Wending our way through the dining room, we dabbed our eyes and fanned blotchy faces. Nearby diners, forks poised in mid-air, stared at this strange procession.

Wayne briefed our hostess on our need for privacy, and she seated us at a corner table on the terrace. Chippendale-styled window boxes overflowing with bright red geraniums and trailing ivy surrounded us. Dark green awnings embossed with huge white Queensbury Qs provided shade.

As we looked at the menus, I glanced over the top of mine at Crandall Park across the street. Summer blooms overflowed their beds. The picturesque white bandstand stood vacant and quiet in the afternoon sun, just as it had all the summers of my youth. The scent of fresh-cut lawns wafted toward us on the breeze. I loved my life, and I thanked God for it as I sat surrounded by favorite people, seeing this old city again through red-rimmed but lucid eyes.

A dozen times, I thanked the wonderful couple who had done so much for Joel and me. As I looked at Maurie, memories of that cold winter resurfaced: being so frightened but putting on a brave face for the world. Feeling so alone, until he brought me home to their sanctuary; the warmth Pam wrapped around my aching heart. Fresh tears drizzled down my cheeks as I expressed the love of my fulfilled role of motherhood and that I owed it all to them. At last, I finished crying and began to celebrate being with my friends.

Pam told us how much she loved both Joel and his brother, Ross. She shared her worry about attending the anniversary party planned for her brother and his wife. Since she hadn't been close to Bill in years, she feared her presence might somehow take away from the party atmosphere.

"Put those feelings aside and go for Joel's sake, Pam. He really wants you there," I said.

Much too soon Pam and Maurie left to continue their journey. I laughed in the parking lot at all the camping gear stuffed in the back of their van and waved as they pulled away.

Our New York vacation sped by, and every family member expressed their delight in my revelation of Joel. Stephanie and I invited my step-mom for lunch one day, promising her a big surprise. Marianne waited eagerly for me to unravel this mystery and wanted me to tell her about it before we even ordered lunch. I could tell she was shaken as she greeted the news with disbelief that I hadn't told my dad. She asked several times why I didn't come to them for help.

"Marianne, there wasn't anything anyone else could do for me."

"But your dad and I could've sent you money or something. It's just terrible you struggled alone like that."

"Money wouldn't have solved anything for me in the short term. I believed with my whole heart that giving my baby to someone else to love was the best thing for him, and that was what mattered most."

In that little German restaurant, we each felt the heavy loss of my father as I described Joel to Marianne. Her eyes misted with tears as I spoke of Joel's love for so many things Dad esteemed—dogs, the outdoors, being out on the water. I knew how close they would've been if they'd met. I envisioned them tramping through high grass across a field, heads cocked toward one another in deep discussion, Dad's English setter bounding ahead, seeking an elusive ring-necked pheasant.

We spent several afternoons on Dale's boat on our beloved Lake George. He and I relived aloud a few youthful adventures of long-past summers at our Dunham's Bay cottage. He treated us to wonderful meals, often at the Algonquin, an old boathouse converted years earlier into a popular restaurant.

When the boat slowed to pass between close islands, Stephanie and I leaned over the side and peered into crystalline emerald water to see rocks and sand, every bottom detail visible ten feet below.

Later, Wayne and I smiled at Stephanie—face shining with happiness—as her favorite uncle leaned over to fine-tune her first-time boat driving. Dale kept us enthralled with tales of the rich and famous owners of ten- to twenty-room "camps" along the shores; some from the 1800s, others of present day millionaires. Bright green lawns sloped gently down to docks and boathouses adorned with artful window boxes full of summer flowers looking like colorful, quizzical eyebrows.

On our last evening, Dale treated twenty-two family members to a Lake George dinner cruise on a brand-new tour boat. Professional singers, he and Pam led the family in an exuberant and harmonized, "Happy birthday, dear Donna," as the ship's waiters, with a grand flourish, set down a huge cake on the buffet. As other guests on the cruise shared my cake, some professed they'd been afraid the windows of the glassed-in lounge would shatter from the sheer volume of the Granger clan's beautiful rendition. My dad would have loved every minute of the day.

The absence of my sons, Shelley, Mandy, and Stephanie's Kevin, marred this perfect trip, but its images imprinted my heart forever.

• • •

After we returned to Texas, Joel told me he'd mailed his parents the letter about finding me. "I'm nervous about Mom's reaction. I know Dad'll be okay, but I won't be able to get a real read on Mom until I hear her voice."

The next night, he said he'd spoken to his mom and dad. They'd received the letter, and I could hear his elation as he described their acceptance and curiosity. He looked forward more than ever to seeing them in September. He was anxious to answer their questions in person.

Wayne and I hadn't shared my news with anyone in his family yet. His annual reunion with his four brothers and families was held every July—this year at Ron's. I could hardly wait to get there so I could tell Ron about Joel.

Since we seldom saw Wayne's other brothers, I was reluctant to share my news with them. Although we'd been married twenty-two years, at times in this very large family I still felt like an outsider, and I feared their reactions.

At Ron's, Wayne and I had a brief opportunity to sit at a picnic table and tell him in private what had happened to me a month earlier. His face lit up in pleasure, but before he could say a word or ask any questions, someone approached, and he deftly changed the topic.

As we left that evening, Ron gave me a warm, longer-than-usual hug. To my surprise he whispered, "I remember you telling me about your baby years ago and thinking then, this is going to somehow have a good ending. I'm so happy for you." Although we'd not worked together for twenty-some years, that instant reminded me of his compassion and why his patients had loved him so much.

I didn't talk to anyone else in Wayne's family about our joyful news for several more weeks. I still wasn't ready to reveal my heart.

Chapter Twenty-Six

Joel and I wished the time between the present and his August visit could somehow fly faster and disappear. We still cried when we talked on the phone, but my tears tasted less of salt as we shared favorite memories of our first weekend. After three incredibly long weeks, he came.

We spent glorious days at the lake together—just the two of us—no interruptions, no entertaining. We spent blissful sunny days and long evenings discovering all we'd missed in the years we'd been apart.

I could not comprehend that although I thought about my son almost every day from the time he was little, he'd determined he would find me. Tears sprang to my eyes each time I envisioned a scene from his twenty-year search. I tried to see things from his side—the phone calls, the disappointments at each dead end. Repeatedly I thanked God for not allowing him to give up.

Joel cooked one of my favorite dishes using his mom's delicious lasagna recipe. As he worked, I sat at our island and told him family stories.

Joel honored my request to bring snapshots from his childhood and we sat on the couch after dinner and looked at each one. I couldn't believe I was seeing my son for the first time as a surfboard-riding four-year-old, an eight-year-old high on a snow bank, bundled up against winter winds as a pre-teen, astride a snowmobile as a teenager.

I tried to memorize each image and mentally placed him along-side his siblings as the three of them grew. I conjured up three freckled noses perched on flushed faces surrounded by sweat-plastered-down curly hair. I saw them crowding in to the kitchen seeking chocolate chip cookies and cold milk after a let's-see-who-gets-the-most-goals game in the back yard. Their much-loved soccer would always be a common denominator. I smiled to myself as I pictured who would be assigned the role of goalie—that's what kid sisters were for, wasn't it? My reverie lasted mere seconds, but more like it came often these days.

I had no doubts Joel's parents raised him in a loving home and gave him benefits only two parents could provide. The more I learned about Joel, the more I confirmed my choice as the right one for him. Even if I could somehow alter my life, I wouldn't change anything in Joel's.

Still, seeing all I'd missed of him was difficult. I asked if I could keep a few of his baby pictures.

"Of course, Mom. Help yourself."

I took a large stack. I had a plan for those photos.

I'm sure my audacity shocked him, but he never said a word.

Wayne and his long-time friend, Bob, joined us Friday night. We spent two days laying flooring in the new cottage next door. Without experience, Wayne and I worked as runners while Bob installed the flooring. Joel cut slate tiles for the fireplace hearth and then started mitering shoe molding for the kitchen and dining room floors. His Seabee construction skills showed as he measured and cut, measured and cut.

Kneeling in the sawdust at the miter saw on the deck, Joel looked up at me and grinned. "Don't tell Shelley I'm doing this, Mom—I still haven't finished our trim work at home."

I brought out an old sled from the storage building, and Joel hung the Royal Flyer from the kitchen ceiling as a pot rack. It's the first thing my guests notice as they enter the kitchen, and everyone compliments its novelty. I can't look at the sled without smiling too. My thoughts aren't so much on the sled as on the one who placed it there.

Joel told me he and Shelley were considering taking two new foster children. Years before, when they first became foster parents, they set a mutual goal to provide a warm, welcoming, and stable haven for children brought to them in crisis.

As sometimes happens in state systems, this time they received little background information except that these boys, aged ten and twelve, who were not siblings had been in the same homes for a number of years. This lack of detail triggered an alarm in their minds, especially with the request for immediate placement. Joel and Shell had been down this red-flag-bedecked road in the past. Nevertheless, they'd met with the caseworker.

On the other hand, the children's stay was supposed to be short—just a couple of weeks. One evening after Joel had talked on the phone to Shelley, they agreed to take, as she called them, "these two little lads."

I envisioned my expanded role as grandma—and if the boys are still with Joel and Shelley for the holidays, maybe even baking Christmas cookies, wrapping boy toys, buying fun things for Mandy's college digs. I saw myself lugging a huge box addressed to the Johnstone family to our local Pack 'N Mail. Better still, perhaps Wayne and I would spend Christmas in Washington this year. It might even be a white Christmas!

• • •

Wayne and I attended a small nearby church. In May, I'd given praise to God as I told the congregation about twice finding money and then a valuable watch. I disclosed it was my belief these blessings came as a result of my praying the Jabez prayer.

During his visit, Joel thrilled me by accompanying me to church. When the time came for the congregation to share any praises, I shot up my hand before anyone else. I asked our minister if I might come to the front to speak. It was unusual, but he agreed. Joel's head snapped up as I got to my feet and scooted to the aisle.

I stood next to the minister and faced the congregation—many of whom still barely knew me. They were all looking a bit confused at this break in format.

I was no stranger to public speaking, and usually prepared myself well in advance, but that Sunday, my face grew hot, and my knees shook.

I focused on my heart and drew in a long, slow breath, gathering in the peace of the sanctuary. I spoke of what happened so long ago, of my loneliness, and what I felt was unpardonable—sending my own child away from my side.

Some people squirmed—some looked down into their laps—a few looked at me with compassion. I spoke of God's grace, forgiveness, and love. As I talked, complete physical and spiritual calm settled on my shoulders. I felt God's love for me, a sinner, humbled and contrite before my brethren.

Not long after our first phone call, Joel sent me his favorite song, explaining it helped sustain him during his search for me—"I Know You're Out There Somewhere" by the Moody Blues. I *did* hear his voice, and he *did* come back to me. The night I received his CD, I wrote a poem. I had no doubt it wasn't my hand doing the writing that night—it poured out of me. In total peace, in front of the congregation, I read it in public for the first time.

"I Know You're Out There Somewhere"

Back then, I couldn't keep you in my arms
Looking ahead, I could see only all the harms
Life seemed so interminably unjust
Your safety was paramount; an absolute must

You were so small and cried to me
Alone, I railed against God in my guilt-ridden sea
I heard you every night, crept toward you, but still—
A million tears, a million prayers, until…

Until this, until that, but no
I could not take it back—it was so
I made a choice—it was finally done
You'd have a dad; to another mother's arms you'd run

The months flew by, and then the years
Blessed with love and joy, it seems we still shed tears
Both flowing west, both swept farther and farther apart
If I could only have told you Joel, I kept you in my heart

You were surrounded by those who loved you
Yet, deep inside, somehow it seems you knew
You plunged ahead, and proudly always did your best
You began a search and would not, *could not* let it rest

I, too, had work, and home, and love, and joy
Wonderful men who loved me; a girl, another boy
I didn't have the right to ask for anything more
Still, alone in the dark, unbidden tears would pour

Your song says, "I know you're out there somewhere"
To ask if you were healthy, safe, or even loved was unfair
You believed it; your faith kept you
knowing that somehow you'd see
I should have known—only God knew the
timeline to bring you back to me
And now your quest is over and
we're bound together tight
We can talk, and laugh and share our
thoughts almost every night
You found me! You came to me!
You swore we'd never part
Best of all—I can hold you, and show
you I kept you in my heart

They stand by and watch us cry, and
wait with love off in the wings

215

I pray someday we can repay those
who watch as our spirit sings
We owe such thanks to our families,
and all the others whom we love
Most of all, my son in my heart, we owe
our thanks to our Father above

And now you know. I've always loved you, Joel. Always.
Mom

When I finished, I looked up at Joel and introduced my son—this most wondrous blessing from God—to the congregation. The sniffles, which began to crescendo midway through my testimony, drowned in a long applause. At the end of the service, it seemed every member of the church shook Joel's hand after hugging Wayne and me.

Our parting again mixed sweet and sorrow but seemed a little less difficult than before. We knew we'd see each other in October when Joel came to Houston for his welding re-certification class.

Every night, thankfulness filled my prayers. My waiting had ended at last and I stayed in a perpetual celebratory mood.

The phone calls between Washington and Texas resumed. Joel and I talked about his upcoming trip to New York for his parents' anniversary party. At times we sat in silence, neither willing our conversation to end. We detailed expansive plans for our first Thanksgiving celebration.

But even plans put in motion sometimes get derailed.

CHAPTER TWENTY-SEVEN

The imminent arrival of two new foster children put enormous pressure on both Joel and Shelley, but especially her. In less than a week, they needed to acquire the boys' school records, complete registration, and purchase school supplies plus extra groceries. The house needed minor adjustments to enable each boy to have his own room. Thanks to her flexible work schedule and understanding bosses, Shelley threw herself into the preparations.

Joel looked forward to the boys' youth soccer and basketball games as well as nightly practices in his back yard. He'd already told me, "Mom, at my house, soccer's not an elective, it's mandatory." He sounded ferocious until he started laughing, and I knew he'd make their home games fun.

Shelley assured me of Joel's level of expertise and dedication to providing much attention to his new pupils. "Most likely the boys will end up as soccer studs with skills far beyond average."

Four days passed without my usual calls from Joel, but I expected his new family was adjusting and blending. His call on Tuesday to describe the first weekend with their charges delighted me.

When the boys arrived, an evening at the pizza parlor got every-one off to a humorous start. Mandy bet all the money in her purse that neither boy dared eat crushed red pepper from the shaker on their table. She didn't quite appreciate how far boys will sometimes go to prove a point—or to win cash. When one of them completed the challenge of eating a teaspoon of red pepper flakes, despite her protests, Joel made sure she paid up. Every cent.

As he relayed this story, his somber tone didn't quite match the details. He didn't say much about their Labor Day weekend of camping. After a few more minutes of innocuous chit chat, I discovered why.

Joel had received word that he'd go from reserve status to active duty.

He'd be leaving for the Naval Amphibious Base in San Diego in a few weeks, and from there serve six months deployed overseas; the strongest rumors suggested in Iraq.

"Mom, when I told Shell I'd gotten recalled again, she just fell apart in front of me. She was angry, crying, and yelling, all at the same time. It went on for hours, and I couldn't do anything for her. It was the worst day of our lives—it was horrible. I don't ever want to see that happen to her again."

He'd also called his dad with the news, and they both predicted his mom would be a basket case all over again—just as she'd been during his deployment in 2001. "Mom stayed upset and worried the whole time I was away. At least with the anniversary party coming up, I'll get to see her before I leave.

"I knew you probably weren't going to be thrilled with the news either, Momma, but I just couldn't face telling you about it yesterday. That's why I didn't call."

The news devastated me. It seemed so unfair to be just beginning to grasp the loveliness of having Joel in my life, to be talking to him every day, and knowing he lived just a four-hour plane ride away. I could almost feel the blood empty from my heart when I thought of him in Iraq.

I knew a lot about Iraq. Like thousands of other mothers, I'd studied Iraq using newspapers, television, and e-mails. I learned about the war, the politics, and the desperate Iraqi soldiers the hard way from a very reliable, in-country source—Jonathan.

The horrors of Jonathan in constant danger of sniper fire, responsible for mammoth fuel trucks, often driving three days without sleep flashed before my eyes. I'd existed on a yo-yo diet of e-mail and prayers for seven and a half months. Jonathan returned safely, but he'd been home less than a year.

How could I bear having another beloved son—this one so new and precious to everyone in our family—go there?

"Joel, I am so sorry about Shell and your mom, but please don't worry about me. As long as you have access to e-mail, I can write you every night. If I hear back from you once a week I'll be fine." I couldn't believe these words came out of my mouth.

Joel wasn't worried about his destination, but it now looked as though their foster children would be in their care longer than expected. Neither boy was adjusting well in school or at home. Leaving Shelley with such a challenging responsibility really frustrated Joel.

Shelley and Joel both felt the kids couldn't afford to miss even one day of school, and a short three-day trip to Texas for five people was too expensive. Because of the many uncertainties, we cancelled plans for our first Thanksgiving.

Some say only infants look forward to a change.

I felt very grown up.

• • •

"Donna, thanks to you and Joel, we're family again." Pam called, sounding very happy. "Despite my misgivings, our differences dissolved and I felt at ease with my brother. I'm so glad I went."

From all accounts, Joel's parents' anniversary party went well. Afterward, Joel spent a night at Pam's home visiting with his cousins.

Joel took his mom to her first Buffalo Bills football game. He'd procured great seats and seeing the players up close thrilled her. Hearing this, I have to admit, I felt a teensy bit jealous—after all, I'd been a Bills fan since before he was born. Jack Kemp was their quarterback when I worked in the nursery at Buffalo General Hospital.

I couldn't resist a little ribbing. "Do you know, Joel, how lucky you are to have *two* mothers who love antiques and are both dyed-in-the-wool Bills fans?"

I loved hearing his deep laugh.

. . .

Joel told me that he and Shelley returned to Washington after their New York vacation, refreshed and eager to begin life with new foster boys. Years of foster parenting prepared them for some of the upheaval in the children's lives, as well as in their own. Even so, summons to the elementary school and neighborhood incidents involving one or both boys occurred more often than they anticipated. To their credit, they remained calm and patient. They set rules, listened, and made themselves available. They voiced their frustrations with the boys' frequent behavior problems only to each other.

Meanwhile, Shelley e-mailed that Mandy exhibited a new, fierce possessiveness of Joel. Angry and tearful, she often told Shelley how much she'd missed him three years earlier during his deployment following 9/11. She made it clear she resented sharing Joel with the boys. In her usual outspoken and dramatic style, she told Joel their behavior was "inexcusable." She thought he and Shelley ought to send them back to where they came from so "we can spend our last few weekends together."

I envisioned Joel's smile as he dismissed her outburst and reminded her that her behavior had been "far worse" when she came to them. As he spoke, his concern centered on Shelley having to deal with so many issues by herself while he was away.

. . .

In October, Joel came to see us in Houston a few days before his welding recertification class began. A friend and long-time coworker would join him in a few days.

Joel picked up a rental car and followed me as I navigated Houston's busy freeways. I hated driving the frenzied loop and led him instead onto the less-traveled toll road. I glanced in the mirror. The day glowed bright and sunny. Seeing Joel's handsome face shielded from the glare by his sunglasses in the car behind me, I felt ebullient, fresh, and alive. I wanted to stop, pull the cars around me aside, and reveal my story to the world. I wanted a sign in every window of my car: "The handsome guy in the car behind me is my *son*."

I stopped at the first of three tollbooths, and of course, paid for the guy behind me—Joel. As I pulled away, I could see him chatting with the booth operator. After each booth, I had to slow the car until he caught up with me. Witnessing his friendliness, I smiled with pride. We headed south toward Stephanie's apartment. As we walked to her door, I asked him what took him so long at the tollbooths.

"I was paying for the guy behind me, Mom. Just like you!"

God's response to my prayers spread my territory, and my heart sang.

I planned to take Joel to Lake Jackson that afternoon, thinking he might like to see where his siblings had grown up.

"Mom, if you don't mind, I'd much rather have time with Stephanie. Can't we spend the day helping her move?"

Out of the mouths of babes. Of course—new family relationships were much more important than real estate. His good sense inspired me.

Stephanie and Joel fell into an instant ease, picking up where they'd left off in July. She took his brotherly ribbing about all the "stuff" she'd accumulated with her usual good nature. At lunchtime they hauled the third truckload toward her new home.

I followed behind in my car, relishing a maternal voyeurism. Through the truck window ahead, I could see them—sometimes with their heads thrown back in laughter, other times in animated discussion—all the while smiling when they looked at one another.

After the recertification class, Wayne, Stephanie and I joined Joel and his coworker Bill, for a fun-filled dinner. As we walked back to our cars later, Bill took me aside.

"You know, Donna, everybody at work loves Joel. We've been close friends a long time, and he's always been a super-great guy. The amazing thing for me is to see the change in him since he found you. He's so happy now—like he's in total peace."

I felt the same happiness, and I knew what he meant by "peace."

• • •

During a phone conversation about favorite movies, Joel told me of his empathy for the young sailor in the movie, *Antwone Fisher*. He'd watched the movie several times and always hoped that one day his story might end like the movie.

Someone murders Antwone's father before his son is born. Antwone is born while his mother serves time for another crime and lives in a foster home. In the opening scenes of the movie, he dreams of a long table laden with food and meeting his kin.

Raised by a minister and his abusive wife, Antwone suffers under their care. As a teenager, he flees the foster home and lives as best he can manage. He grows into an angry young man and joins the navy where he often acts out his rage. As part of his punishment for fighting, he struggles through months of therapy. He cannot understand why his mother never came for him after her release from prison. The therapist helps him realize he must refocus his life. At the end of the movie, he searches and finally meets his father's family. As he circles a large table covered in dishes heaped with food, outstretched arms and smiling faces surround him.

I did my best to surprise Joel with his own Antwone Fisher moment while he visited. That evening, we walked into a restaurant to meet Wayne for dinner. Dozens of our friends seated along a stretch of barbecue-laden tables greeted Joel with hugs, handshakes, and more than a few misty eyes.

• • •

Most of me felt a sunny contentment now, but the shadow of Joel going to war clouded parts of every day with intermittent worries. As our third too-quick weekend ended, both Wayne and I hated to see him leave, not knowing when we'd be together again.

CHAPTER TWENTY-EIGHT

Joel's orders required him to report to San Diego for warfare weaponry training. Uncertain of his deployment date and final destination, he assured us he'd fulfill his duty. "If I'm being taken away from my family again, in a way, I do hope I'm sent to Iraq. I want to contribute something to this war."

I loved that Joel could be so honest with me, but his statement launched a rocket into my chest. I could only imagine what it did to Shelley—if he'd shared this thought with her at all.

In Thailand in 2002, Joel had provided support services to Navy Seals in their training exercises with Thai Seals. Now, official word came down that command would again need a mature, experienced Seabee. His commanding officer must have heard my prayers—Joel would return to Thailand for six months.

I'd understood Joel's patriotism; in fact, I lauded it. Still, as his mother I didn't feel one bit selfish when I rejoiced in the fact he wasn't going to Iraq. I felt certain Joan and the tight circle of others who loved him were all just fine with his current orders, too.

From e-mails, I knew Shelley saw Joel's agony over leaving her with their new obligations. She told me she hated that he was going away, but in spite of the challenges, she steeled herself to care for the boys alone.

Joel packed his old Ford Bronco for the lonely 1300-mile drive down the West Coast to San Diego. He called me on the way. I could hear the angst in his voice as he spoke of Shelley, saying she assured him she could handle things on the home front. I'm sure she displayed a granite-like exterior, while inside it must have taken all her inner strength to hide the truth as quicksand covered her broken heart.

• • •

Once in San Diego, Joel spent weeks rotating through classes, organizing warehouses, and preparing pallets of troop supplies to ship around the world. He learned the intricacies of stacking and balancing tons of hazardous materials in huge cargo planes.

He complained of too much down time and not enough work to make full use of his days. Determined to stay fit, he worked out, lifting weights every day, running the beach in front of the beautiful old Del Coronado Hotel, taking advantage of a few nearby golf courses on the weekends.

In e-mails, I repeated my questions about his deployment date—I hated the uncertainty of his departure for Thailand. Patient, he explained the anticipated routine. He'd be in San Diego for weeks, then Thailand for six months, and then return to San Diego until he'd completed a year of active duty.

I hurried to finish his Christmas present before he left the States. I took 125 photographs, thirty captions, and one song request to a photo service, requesting a rush job. Moved by our story and this first Christmas present to my son, the processors surpassed my expectations of expediency. Two days later, I picked up four identical DVDs.

I wanted him to see my project *now*—in case his orders moved up his deployment. I overnighted one to Joel and called to tell him to open his present as soon as it arrived. He balked.

"Mom, I'm going to wait. I'm pretty sure I'll be able to get home to Washington for Christmas."

"But, honey, I don't want you to wait. I'm too excited."

The DVDs contained blended shots of our family and Joel set to music. Spanning 1909 to 2004, the pictures began with my grandparents holding my parents as infants, progressed through my childhood, and on to the present. As my children grew, the photos revealed them enjoying similar activities at the same ages—swimming, playing ball, riding horses. The team uniforms differed, but the curly hair, freckled noses, and smiles looked alike.

The background music suited the times depicted—big band sounds for early scenes of my dad and mom, "Sunshine on My Shoulder Makes Me Happy" for Stephanie and Jonathan's youth, and "I Know You're Out There Somewhere" for many of Joel's photos. Fitting words and music, "We Are Fam-i-ly" spun around the last scene, our July Fourth family portrait.

Joel called to cry with me. The gift impressed and touched him, and he said he was thrilled to have it to take overseas. "That is, if I don't wear it out first, Mom."

He joined Shelley and the children for Thanksgiving and made his last trip home to Washington toward the end of December. A frenzied Christmas, with the two boys exuberant over their bevy of gifts, left the house a happy wreck. Three days later, emotional chaos reigned as Joel left again for San Diego.

His next flight would last twenty-two hours. It sounded as though Thailand was at the end of the world.

For me, it was.

. . .

I could read the sadness between the lines of Shelly's e-mails and knew she struggled with being apart from Joel. I imagined her alone, braving each day in her confined world of work and the boys. From my perspective, Joel's time in Thailand didn't qualify as a nightmare, but a daydream in which I plodded through the wet, sucking sands of an endless beach.

Joel kept us all going—Shelley, his parents, and me—with e-mails and occasional cell phone calls. He wrote and called Shelley's mom and Mandy as well, but communication failed to close the distance. In spite of the time zone difference, I assured Joel he could call me anytime, day or night.

One night he called at 2:30 a.m. I pretended I'd been awake, but I'm sure my voice betrayed drowsy confusion because Joel laughed.

"You said I could call anytime, right, Mom?" He described a bay near Phukett—where he and his Thai guide stood in a long, narrow aqua-colored boat—hiding from the Seal team whose practice search and destroy mission was to find him. "It's just so beautiful, Mom. The sun's going down, the water's calm, and I just had to share it with you. I know you'd love seeing it."

We talked for a while, and smiling, I went back to sleep. Fortunately, Wayne was working in Houston, because Joel called back half an hour later. He described more color changes—a coral sun drifting off the horizon into an incredible turquoise sea. *God's artwork. I'm so glad Joel notices it too.*

Many times in the past year, we'd marveled at seeing the same sun, the same moon, but from different vantage points. When he'd called me from home, Joel sat outside on his steps to escape the boys' noise.

As we talked, I often stepped outside to look at the stars and moon from our deck. Every few minutes I could hear the little whoomph in his voice as he threw a ball for Josie, his chocolate Lab. I could hear Shelley running water, the metallic clack of a replaced pot lid, and the children's voices farther away. The miracle of cell phone technology made me feel as though his deck was next door, and I reveled in the sounds of his life.

All around me, spring's beautiful dogwood show passed by. White blossoms fluttered to the ground, leaving behind bright green unfurling leaves. I loved the warming of the days, the sunrises, like sherbet-colored silk scarves spreading across the shimmering lake.

I kept myself busy, working, writing daily e-mails to Joel—marking time. I finalized plans for a summer trip to New York. I lived a happy life filled with love, but I missed Joel every day. Almost as much as the lengthening days, I relished every setting sun, whose glazed glow brought me one day closer to Joel's return.

I needed my family support system around me, and Jonathan, Kevin, and Stephanie came for Memorial Day weekend. Jonathan began building a much-needed deck outside a storage building. Stephanie and Kevin helped, and I smiled as I listened to construction sounds coming through my screen door. Their easy banter mixed with the whines of the saw, the sharp report of a hammer, and the whir of a drill.

I e-mailed photos of their progress to Joel, and his reply revealed how much he wanted to be here helping.

Jonathan's newfound building skills made us all proud. Working from a plan he drew up after reading a deck-building book, he labored long into each night to finish. Although he'd never built anything before, Jonathan's deck turned out to be both beautiful and functional, with a ramp for Wayne to drive his motorized wheelbarrow up to the shed doorway.

· · ·

Wayne surprised me with a homerun Mother's Day gift—tickets to a Moody Blues concert in Dallas on June 17—one year to the day since Joel's first call to me. It didn't matter we sat in the nosebleed section because hearing the group sing Joel's favorite song, "I Know You're Out There Somewhere" thrilled me at any distance.

I resisted a tremendous urge to rush down to the front to tell the band how much the song meant to my son and me. Wayne said he had the same urge. Instead, we just cried and clapped. We held hands leaving the concert, congratulating each other with one of my favorite expressions—we'd used "admirable restraint."

· · ·

Time for Wayne's family reunion rolled around again—this one at his brother's home outside of Buffalo. By now, no longer fearing their response, I'd e-mailed his three other brothers and given them the details of Joel's finding me. They seemed sincerely interested and I'd kept them abreast of Joel's reactivation and packed photos to share during our Saturday picnic.

I'd e-mailed Pam we'd be in the Buffalo area and wanted to stop by for a visit. Ever the consummate hosts, she and Maurie insisted Wayne and I not only stay with them during the reunion weekend but also extend our visit by several days.

Following Pam's directions, we drove down a shady tree-lined avenue. I didn't remember many things about the neighborhood. We passed a large old park bordered by well-kept lawns. Three-story dignified homes, many with flags tilting out from their deep porches, sat in silent homage to long ago days of quiet wealth. With their Painted-Lady Victorian hues, each house fought to take center stage, like understudies stealing scenes. The street looked like photos from a beautiful patriotic calendar.

A few houses later, I recognized Pam's beckoning front porch and her parents' house across the street. I hurried up the steps toward the open front door and called through the screen. I heard Pam and Maurie's voices as they came through the hallway, and even though they weren't to the entryway yet, I burst inside and rushed to the arms of my dear friends.

We picked up the threads of our lives where we'd left them a year earlier in Glens Falls. As Pam and I talked, Maurie's ready laughter rang through the large rooms, filled to bursting with antiques. I surveyed beautiful chests and tables, all without blemish. Old china plates marched around a plate rail at the top of the dining room walls. As at my mother's, Pam had clear, colored dishes resting atop the window ledges, sparkling in the summer sunshine. Beside Pam's chair sat an old peddler's cart, filled with videos, magazines, and children's toys.

While we recounted memories from our shared past, Wayne whispered, "I see how easy it is for you to love these people. I feel as though I've known them for years."

Despite an oppressive heat wave, Wayne and I spent cool nights under air conditioning in *my* old bedroom. The floor still groaned in the same places, the door gave forth the same hollow clunk when it latched.

Across from my doorway at the top of the stairs was the infamous laundry chute down which Joel had stuffed his baby cousin. The stairs at both ends of the house still released their sonorous creaks. I joked that Maurie maintained the creaks to keep any of the Dewey kids from sneaking in late.

One morning, I tagged along with Maurie as he watered his hundreds of plants, loving his on-going lessons in gardening, antiques, and history. He pointed to an old carriage in his garage in the alley behind his house. "All these garages served as carriage houses one hundred years ago." His images of life then were so real I envisioned grooms gossiping with each other as they unhitched lathered horses from shiny black carriages.

One alley held secrets of its own. After I'd delivered, when Pam visited me in the hospital, she brought her sister-in-law to see the baby boy she and Bill would soon adopt. For weeks afterward, the alley across the street hid the comings and goings of Joan and Bill as they brought their new son to visit his grandparents without creating the possibility of me seeing them.

The heat wave lasted for days. We enjoyed the Paul family reunion but were happy to return to Pam and Maurie's in the evenings. It was too hot to cook, so we enjoyed a few meals of local foods I'd almost forgotten—roast beef piled high on crusty salted rolls, marvelous Italian dishes, and ice cream with dark chocolate orange sauce.

After dinner one evening, Pam reclined in her red leather chair. Maurie lounged in his dark brown one, and Wayne and I sat together on the sofa. Piles of medical journals and legal-sized tablets of notes were stacked on Maurie's ottoman. The room had more antiques in it now.

I began to tell Wayne some of the things I remembered from my stay with the Deweys, and they took turns sharing some of their stories with us. Pam started by talking about her husband. Without contemplation, Maurie brought home neglected children and abandoned babies, some for a night or two, some for months. On several occasions, he called her from the hospital to come pick up babies and toddlers in the wee hours of the morning. She'd always wanted six children, and they had four boys. They adopted two girls from the waifs brought to them for foster care, one of whom was Sarah.

One of Maurie's unusual tales involved a young physician whose wife was four days post-partum and scheduled for discharge the next morning. As Maurie made evening rounds, he found her in tears and asked her what was wrong.

The overwrought mother insisted she couldn't allow her husband, even if he *was* a physician, to be near her baby. "He doesn't know a thing about babies," she sobbed.

Maurie reassured her, "I can fix that. Your husband and the baby can come to our house tonight, and Pam will teach him everything he needs to know."

As promised, under Pam's tutelage, the doctor-dad learned to feed, change, and bathe his new baby in one evening. Mom, dad, and baby went home together the next morning, each secure and happy in their new roles.

I realized these rescues were a pattern in the Dewey household. I recalled how quickly Maurie offered their home to me and shuddered many times over the next few decades at the realization of what might have happened to me without their help. At the time, I was so despaired of my situation, I'd never asked him, why me?

During the past year, though, I'd wondered how Maurie decided his wife's family should adopt *my baby*. I had dark hair, like Pam and her brother, and we were all of Scottish heritage—maybe that was it. On the other hand, was it something else? Had Joan and Bill been seeking a baby to adopt? I hoped Maurie's answer wasn't that he felt sorry for me, but I had to ask.

Maurie said, "Your buddies on the floor told me about your home life when I started hospital rounds that evening."

When he came into the nursery and saw me so visibly upset, he decided what he thought would be best for me. Without even a phone call, he felt certain Pam would agree they should take me into their home.

Why my baby went to someone in Pam and Maurie's family was still not clear. Surely, there were other babies available from women more educated, more refined, or better known to them. I came right out and asked, "Maurie, did you see me as a pretty girl or think I was a good nurse? Did you feel I was a little above average in intelligence?"

Perhaps he felt I would deliver a handsome, smart child. He knew I loved the babies in our nursery—maybe he thought I would pass on my loving nature.

His bright eyes twinkled behind his glasses. "Oh, I don't know— you were just in the right place at the right time."

"Oh, no, Maurie, I want a better reason than that!"

Next to him, I noticed Pam's eyes welling up. Maurie looked at me. "Donna, don't you know yet? It was all of those things."

Chapter Twenty-Nine

I imagined driving from Rochester to Pam and Maurie's to meet *her*—the one Joel also called mom—must be a hard trip for Joel's parents. Although Joan and I had recently begun to e-mail one another, we didn't know each other and were still virtual strangers. They knew I'd lived with Pam and Maurie, but beyond that I couldn't be sure what else they knew.

I didn't know how their past relationship with Pam and Maurie had been. Joel told me he and Ross played with cousins when he was young but not later. I couldn't recall Pam talking much about her brother and his wife when I lived with them. Perhaps she'd mentioned them in conversation and I'd forgotten. Or maybe she omitted more than a mere mention for another purpose. Although their relationship was none of my concern, I believed it affected how today's meeting could go.

I felt anxious and a little afraid of Bill and Joan's potential feelings toward me. They might perceive me as an intruder into their past, sneaking like a muddy dog into their present, or as someone wishing to steal their future with their beloved Joel. As a mother, I understood how easily Joan, in particular, might experience these fears.

Pam and I ran a few errands, picking up last minute groceries. Fully expecting we would return in time for me to re-shower and change into a dressier outfit, I saw an unfamiliar car parked in front of the house. Confirming my fears, Pam said, "Oh good, they're here early."

Joan stood at the trunk of her car. Shorter than I'd envisioned, this attractive woman had silver hair cut short like mine. She smiled at Pam and me as we climbed out of our van. Joan had beautiful skin and walked toward us with a quick, sure step. With a crew cut like my dad's, tall and slender Bill hung back at first but towered above us when he shook my hand. I wondered if any of them could see the terror I felt.

The four of us carried groceries, suitcases, and a few small bags into the house. Hearing the commotion through the screen door, Wayne came in from the back porch where he'd been reading the Sunday paper. We all chattered nervously, but after a few minutes the strangeness of the initial meeting passed. Now that I'd seen them, I felt even more desperate for both Joan and Bill to like me, and not feel threatened by my discovery and continuing presence.

While Pam and Maurie put groceries away, Wayne retreated to the back porch.

Joan, Bill, and I stood close together on a beautiful antique oriental rug in the living room. Pent-up emotion prevented us from relaxing enough to seat ourselves. Silence fell over us.

I didn't know what to say, so I stared at the pattern beneath my feet and wondered how many times had Joel crawled to Joan on this rug. Had he learned to walk from chair to couch in this room? Had he spilled crumbs from one of his birthday cakes here? Played board games surrounded by his cousins?

Then God whispered the words to express what I'd come all the way from Texas to say. Sharing a lifetime of relief, I thanked them for loving my son and for the many ways their love showed itself in Joel.

In turn, they thanked me for their son. Tears flowed all around.

• • •

Later that evening we sat on white wicker furniture on the deep front porch. We admired Maurie's prolific gardens as we watched him watering. I marveled aloud that he also planted and watered all the plants encircling their block.

As we chatted, it became evident Joan and Bill were a fun-loving couple, how proud they were of Joel, how much they loved both their boys. We drifted from porch to living room, and outside again, seeking relief from the hot, humid weather.

Wayne and Bill hit it off right away and relaxed with Maurie on the back stoop. Pam, Joan, and I laughed about Joel's having *two* mothers who loved antiques, cooking, and the Buffalo Bills. We agreed—how could he be so lucky?

For the remainder of the afternoon, the six of us continued asking questions, talking nonstop about our families, but most often talking about the wonderful young man we'd begun to share. When they spoke of him, their beaming faces brought home a truth about Joel. It takes a whole family to raise a child. Joan and I exchanged gifts and made promises to keep in touch with e-mails.

That evening we set out a huge smorgasbord, our ranks at the large dining table swollen with two of Pam and Maurie's children and their young families. It was a full house—filled with the boisterous noise of adults and babies, laughter, and calm, comfortable love.

Joan served a tray of beautiful browned potato rolls, for which, Bill bragged, she was well known. I thought of Jonathan, who requested potato rolls from my kitchen every holiday. As I buttered the second half of one, a grin grew inside me. While mine tasted sweeter, hers held the perfect shape, which always eluded me.

Joel called from Thailand and chatted with his parents, his aunt and uncle, two cousins, Wayne, and then me. From his quiet sniffle, I knew tears ballooning with joy, anxiety, and love spilled down faces on both ends of the conversation.

Pam brought out a large birthday cake decorated with pale pink piping and roses. The frosting salutation announced the cake celebrated my birthday three days earlier. Forgetting this date was her sister-in-law's birthday, with a flourishing "ta-dahhh" Pam set the cake in front of me. Joan demonstrated what a good-sport looks like as she dissolved everyone's embarrassment. She carved her name beside mine in the frosting, popped a large finger-scoopful into her mouth and proclaimed, "Our cake is delicious!"

Late that evening, Maurie carried emptied glasses to Pam and Joan in the kitchen, and Wayne headed upstairs.

In a quiet moment, Bill and I stood alone in the living room. He draped his arm around my shoulders. I looked up, a little surprised but pleased at this gentle touch. "Donna, I've been watching you all day."

Very much aware his gaze had followed me, I nodded.

"It's easy to see where Joel gets his sweetness."

The next day, we took pictures on the back porch. Joan and I stood beside one another. Wayne and Pam sat in chairs, and Bill and Maurie stood at the back of the group. The smiles on each face looked totally genuine in the digital photographs. Amid warm embraces, we thanked each other repeatedly as Wayne and I said our good-byes to Joel's mom and dad.

Peace filled my heart when I reflected upon the visit. I now knew I'd received much more from Pam and Maurie than their loving shelter and comfort. Even if I'd had all the resources in the world at my fingertips, I could never have found better parents for my son.

Joel e-mailed from Thailand, still apprehensive. I assured him I'd only one regret—the visit was too short. Leaving new friends was just as hard as leaving Pam and Maurie.

CHAPTER THIRTY

By the time Joel came home from Thailand, both foster boys had gone back to their families. Joel, Shelley, and Mandy flew to Texas for Thanksgiving. Jonathan, Stephanie, and her now-fiancé, Kevin, came as well. Granger Cottage fulfilled its promise to hold my children close and safe.

The lake shimmered outside the porch windows. A constant wind slapped rows of waves against the shore. We stood around a long table set with my mother's beautiful antique dishes. The afternoon sunlight caught the waves, flinging reflections that raced over our water glasses.

I squeezed my husband's hand as I took in each of my children standing side by side. Another dream realized—our first holiday together. Wayne squeezed my hand back, gave me a nudge, and cleared his throat. I bowed my head and forced my eyes closed. He led us in a heartfelt prayer of thanks for *all* the blessings we'd received this year.

Crisp golden-brown skin crackled as Jonathan sliced the turkey. Scents of turkey, gravy, rolls, and apple pie filled the house as serving dishes passed back and forth. Amid plates heaped high with steamy hot food, cranberry-orange relish and fruit salad waited in cut glass bowls. A large basket of potato rolls requested by Jonathan sat there, ready for Joel to experience his other mother's version.

As the rush at food subsided, everyone began to eat more slowly and discuss Stephanie's wedding. She and Kevin wanted a small ceremony in our front yard. They'd set a date in April to be certain Joel's deployment had ended. Our busy weekend overflowed with laughter, food, and a great deal of yard work involving loads of dirt and a borrowed tractor. Joel smoothed the yard for a new lawn and gave all the girls tractor-driving lessons. Jonathan built us a fire pit, and at night we sat on log benches and told ghost stories in the firelight.

Throughout the weekend, my children took turns teasing me. "Did you find Gran yet, Mom?"

I hated having to answer, "Not yet, honey, but I will before the wedding."

From the deck, I watched Joel waterskiing in the late afternoon. He leaned back against the rope, tilting to send a tall rooster tail plume spraying toward the beach. Memories of my youth crowded to the surface—Joel was so like my brother Dale!

It didn't seem as difficult to say good-bye when my children departed. I knew they'd all be back in East Texas in a few months for an even larger celebration.

I put the Blue Onion dishes back in the pine cupboard. I couldn't touch them without thinking of my mother. *Now, God, if you could only help me find her…* I was still asking Him for favors.

At the end of December, Wayne and I spent Christmas in Washington with Joel, Shelley, and Mandy. Even the area's legendary chilly grayness couldn't dampen our holidays. We met one of the boys who'd stayed with them in foster care—the one who'd taken the bet and eaten the pepper flakes. He had an angelic countenance, chattered nonstop, and crept into my heart. He was living again with his mom in a tiny duplex, but Shelley told us that on occasion his behavior reflected the rigors of a troubled life.

Joel and Shelley hosted a large party, and Joel introduced me to many of the friends I'd glimpsed in the photo album Shelly had brought on their first Texas visit. I enjoyed seeing people's reactions when they realized Joel looked so much like me.

Many guests at the party told me Joel was a favorite friend, coworker, or neighbor. I knew enough of him by now to know they were sincere. As I chatted with a group of four men, one asked me, "Was it hard for you to decide about Joel's adoption?"

His forthright question took me by surprise. In the midst of a home decorated for the holidays, crowded with happy people, I revealed a little of my heart. "It was the hardest thing I've ever done in my life. The most important part of all of this is seeing the man Joel's become. *That* makes the sad part of my past irrelevant. His parents did a wonderful thing, raising Joel in a loving home, and I will always love them for it."

My favorite moments of our visit, other than Christmas morning, came in the early mornings. I made myself a cup of orange cappuccino and carried it to the living room where I sat and surveyed Joel's surroundings. Joel came downstairs to join me for a few quiet minutes before leaving for work.

"Joel, this is the sweetest Christmas for both Wayne and me. You and Shelley have become the children we never had together."

• • •

I drove home from the post office, savoring the warm weather and views of the lakeshore. Shades of lavender and brilliant white amid dazzling greens burst forth from wild red bud and dogwood. High in the pines wisteria bloomed purple against a clear blue sky. I slowed the car as I crossed the bridge of Alley Creek. In the distance, a lone angler stood in his boat, silhouetted against the open waters. Close to the shore, shiny black mounds of turtles competed for sunning space on protruding logs.

Stephanie's wedding was in three weeks. Despite my desire to be outdoors, I forced myself to keep working on clearing the enclosed porch where we'd seat the bridal party for dinner. I moved the mundane from boxes on the porch to a proper cupboard or the trash barrel. The stacks of boxes lowered, but I ran out of display and storage room. The boxes, the cleaning, the wedding—it seemed overwhelming. I took a few minutes and propped my feet up on a stool.

Reminding myself I still had work to do, I stood and headed back to the remaining boxes.

I picked up a Dole fruit box, heavy for its size. Inside, paper-wrapped items snuggled like cousins sharing grandma's big bed. A familiar sparkle and an odd texture peeked out from beneath the edge of manila wrapping. I pulled out a chubby, gold-glittered bird of papier-mâché, a heavy cut-glass receptacle for oil in a mahogany sconce, and its mate.

More items from my former living room emerged as wrappings piled up on the floor. The last object stood heavy, held tight to the corner by a small, rounded shape. I slid the smaller piece aside and pulled at the paper on the tall item.

My tears distorted the butterflies, daisies, and sweet peas dancing about a porcelain melon-shaped jar. The sudden pain in my throat caught my breath. I was holding the biscuit jar! Its fluted opening yielded the softest gray contents, secure in a sealed bag.

Momma, oh, Momma. I found you at last. Now, we can do this wedding—now I know you are close in spirit, loving our beautiful Stephanie, knowing everyone will meet Joel, proud of our tall, handsome Jonathan. As the sun sets and the candles lit, your sisters' children and yours, all gray haired now, will reminisce with your grandchildren about how you always enjoyed a party.

• • •

The day before Stephanie's wedding at our house, Dale, Joel, and Jonathan strolled though early morning mists playing their first round of golf together. They never admitted who shot the lowest score. After the rehearsal dinner, we stood around the gleaming mahogany piano Dad bought when Dale was born. Pam and Dale sang "All I Ask of You" from *Phantom of the Opera* for the bride and groom. I beamed with pleasure that Joel heard their voices at last. Pam played a dozen more show tunes, and we all sang. My father would have found such an evening of love and music irresistible.

Late Saturday afternoon, after Jonathan and Joel led guests to their seats, Don escorted our beautiful daughter down the new sloping lawn. Kevin and Stephanie were married, standing with their backs to a tangerine sun setting across the pink and gold lake. They faced a hundred guests, including Dale and his wife, Pam; my sister, Noel; Dale's daughter, Jennifer, and all my New Jersey cousins.

While the bride and groom were busy with photographs, I pulled Joel aside to introduce him to Ron and Carol. In recognition of Joel's recent service to his country, Ron presented him with a flag flown over the Capitol on his birthday. Jonathan beamed with pride at his brother.

Joel embraced me afterward, whispering in his deep, soft voice, "Momma, you keep making me cry…"

Chapter Thirty-One

As I sweep thousands of pine needles from my deck, I pause to look heavenward. Baby blue and delicate pink cotton candy clouds paint the fall sky. Scarlet, bronze, and gold leaves ripple and towering pines sway, showing me the wind's rhythm. As the wind whispers, pine needles fling themselves downward.

The sun silhouettes a large bird into a swift, dark shadow across the roof. Perhaps it's a hawk or one of the rare eagles that settle here in winter. Shivering a little, I sip cooled-off coffee from a bright yellow and turquoise mug from Joan. Along the railings, planters hold rows of tiny, purple-faced violas bending to each other like schoolchildren sharing secrets. By my feet, Danny thumps his tail, watching me expectantly. Vegas dozes belly-up in the grass below the deck, secure in her world that Danny will wake her for any bark-worthy endeavors. Neither dog pays heed to dropping temperatures.

God is doing His deep cleaning, readying the forest for its season of rest. Like autumn's leaves, my cares drift to the ground to crumble into tomorrow's earth. When God revealed part of His plans for me, He put my fears to rest and allowed me to hear His song in every silence. He answered my prayers that Joel's parents love my child and keep him safe. God is my helper and turned my mourning into dancing, put off my sackcloth, and girded me with gladness...

Joel's searching is over, and he now knows my love.

I know my son.

He loves me.

Our bonds are everlasting.

FROM MY PERSPECTIVE
BY JOEL JOHNSTONE

The year I turned five, our family moved to the summer cottage my grandfather built on Lake Ontario. After we moved, our parents told Ross and me we were adopted. Being "adopted" didn't have significance for me—Mom and Dad were my parents, and Ross was my brother. Neither of us had much information about our birth mothers or their circumstances, mostly, I think, because Mom wanted to protect our mothers. I wondered aloud about mine when I was small but later realized I hurt Mom by asking direct questions.

My brother and I knew Uncle Maurie delivered us, but I also knew my birth mother had another connection to him and Aunt Pam. I don't remember asking Aunt Pam about my mother, but she says I did.

As I grew older, sometimes I imagined myself in covert surveillance, watching the woman who gave me life—never speaking to her or even allowing her to see me. I told myself that just seeing her from a distance would be enough to satisfy me. I followed ladies in the mall if they seemed to look or act in some way like me.

As a teenager, I continued fantasizing about finding my mother. I might've mentioned it to friends, but the search lived more in my mind than in reality.

After high school, I joined the navy. I felt independent enough to begin searching in earnest. I visited Uncle Maurie and Aunt Pam to find out the circumstances of my birth. Uncle Maurie said because he was my mother's doctor, it was unethical for him to give me any information. Aunt Pam no longer recalled my mother's maiden name, age, which high school or nursing school she'd attended. She did share one distant memory—that my mother married someone named White and that she'd moved to Washington state.

During the 1990s, Shelley and I lived in Bremerton, Washington. Shelley was incredibly supportive in my search, and we contacted an agency to help find my mother. I also hired a private investigator. Without a correct maiden name or other important facts, their research proved fruitless.

Each time I stopped looking, the vision of seeing my mother haunted me. On my birthdays and Mother's Day, I wondered if she thought about me. Every time I did the math, I wondered, *Is she still alive?* The fear she might be gone spurred me into action, but each avenue I pursued proved empty.

In spring 2004, I called Uncle Maurie and Aunt Pam and each of their six kids to invite them to a fiftieth anniversary party for my parents. I called their youngest daughter, Sarah, and found she'd grown into a lively, curious, young woman. I hadn't seen Sarah since she was a little girl, but something clicked between us that night. We talked on the phone a long time, describing our adult lives and reliving childhood memories. I mentioned searching for the woman who'd lived with her parents before giving birth to me. As an adopted child herself, Sarah immediately volunteered to be the point person for my investigation.

Sarah peppered her mom with questions in hopes of bringing new facts to light. She made phone calls and searched the web. She was very determined that she could help fulfill my wish to find my mother. Aunt Pam helped also, joining a website to seek my mother's classmates, but couldn't make any connections. Even though Sarah called me with frustrating reports, she always had another plan ready. It may have been my dream, but it became Sarah's mission. She refused to give up.

On a Wednesday evening in mid-June that same year, Sarah and Aunt Pam called with news. Sarah had just spoken to my mother!

My stomach clenched—I started to sweat. My hand shook as I scribbled down the name and Texas address. I gripped the receiver harder. My body went numb as Sarah rushed on, relaying the conversation.

"Donna's easy to talk to and seems anxious to connect with you, Joel."

When Sarah paused to catch her breath, Aunt Pam jumped in to tell me how much I looked like my mother. She said she'd often told me that when I was a little boy.

I didn't remember. I'm not sure I remembered much of anything at that point.

All I could think of was the phone call I would make the following night. I understood why my mother told Sarah she couldn't talk to me right away. After all I'd imagined about my mother, I'd no idea what would actually come out of my mouth when I finally spoke with her.

Shelley and I talked long into the night. Over the years, she'd been a rock of support for me. More than anyone, she knew how I longed for a sense of closure. In a leap of blind optimism, we looked at our work schedules to determine when we might travel to Texas *if* my mother agreed to meet us. So much depended on the next day's phone conversation—and the biggest *if* of my life.

Early the next morning I mailed family snapshots to my mother. I drove on autopilot several hundred miles toward my next job site. During the trip, Shelley spoke to me by cell phone and gave me details of e-mails as she and my mother exchanged them. She described pictures of my mother and new brother and sister e-mailed from Texas.

I didn't know so many things about my mother. I had a hundred questions and wanted immediate answers.

As soon as I got to my hotel room, I grabbed my cell phone. I read the number off my scribbled notes. Holding my breath, I punched in each digit of the telephone number: 9-0-3-7...

I heard the call connect, then two rings. I heard my mother's voice—somewhat soft, questioning, yet confident.

"Hello?"

Total relief washed over me. I exhaled, and as though I'd been saying it my entire life, I choked out a greeting. "Hi, Mom. It's Joel."

Neither of us could keep from crying, but within minutes, we laughed over the life details we shared. I don't know how long we spoke, but it seemed somewhere between a few seconds and an entire lifetime. We ended with promises to talk again the next night.

Before I disconnected I asked one last question. "You know I have to meet you, right, Mom?"

"Of course you do."

Hearing her words of assurance, of willingness to meet me brought instant respite. I was jubilant. "That's great, because we're coming in two weeks!"

My mind raced with a hundred more questions as I tossed and turned that night. I replayed the conversation repeatedly in my head. I couldn't wait to hear her voice again.

From then on, Mom and I laughed and cried together every chance we got, e-mailing in between phone conversations. My need to know my mother, her life and my new family was insatiable. Shelley received e-mails from Mom, too, and we shared information every night. The phone calls eased me through the next two weeks.

I wasn't scared about meeting my family for the first time, but I'll admit to being nervous. I drive a lot for work, but the trip from the airport in Dallas to East Texas seemed relentless torture. Eight miles from making my dreams come true; I drove across a bridge at the end of the lake. It was very late at night. The last miles ticked by, and I knew we were close. My head pounded from the tension.

I could hardly breathe. My eyes burned as I searched for the correct turns. I saw truck lights flashing ahead and realized it signaled us. Driver's window down, I recognized Wayne from the pictures I'd studied. He waited for me to pull alongside and motioned me to follow him down a pitch-black road. Each turn in the subdivision, each rise, each dip caused my stomach to roll.

Wayne made a final turn into his driveway.

My heart tore at the constraint of my ribs when I jammed the gearshift into park and jumped out of the rental.

I found my mother, eyes brimming, coming toward me, and we hugged.

I didn't think I could ever let go.

. . .

I always wondered if I had a sister or another brother besides Ross. Not long before sweet Sarah found my mother, I told Shelley of a recent dream. In the dream, I walked toward a pool area to meet my mother, two brothers, and a sister. To discover that *Jonathan and Stephanie* share my mother is an amazing revelation—I *do* have two brothers and a sister.

Jonathan and I are quiet. We share similar tastes in music and a love for soccer and golf. Maybe because I'm a guy or because he didn't know I even existed until I burst into his life, I still worry sometimes about his feelings about me. For his entire life, he was the oldest and the only boy. I don't want him to feel like middle-child Jan of *The Brady Bunch*.

Stephanie's easy to read, and I loved her from the first time I saw her.

That first weekend, Wayne, Jonathan, and Stephanie opened their hearts to me. It still seems awkward at times to be a part of them, but that comes from within, not from anything they express.

My hope is that we can continue to grow closer and strengthen our relationships.

I stalled for a while before I wrote to my parents in New York and finally called them to talk about finding my birth mother. I felt all along that it would be easier for Dad than for Mom. He was accepting and gave his sincere best wishes. While Dad was very happy that we found each other, Mom was quieter. She said she was glad for me, but I worried that deep inside she hurt. Today I share things about my new family if she asks, but I'll always be protective of her feelings.

Our daughter, Mandy, believed in my quest, supporting my efforts in her own teenage way. Shelley and I have many friends who stood by me all those years, encouraging and hopeful of a good outcome. They shared our joy and tears as we spread the news—mission accomplished.

My best friend, Bill, was the first to meet Mom. While he and I were in Texas for a welding certification class, I heard him tell her he'd never seen me happier.

When Mom and Wayne came to Washington for Christmas, friends and coworkers made special efforts to attend our open house to welcome them.

• • •

If I had the opportunity to speak to a pregnant single woman today, I'd encourage her to consider adoption if circumstances prohibit her raising a child alone. Adoption can be a win-win situation all around. Every kid deserves a home. I had a great one, filled with the love of two people who raised me to adulthood. They set concrete examples for marriage and parenting. They will always be my parents. I will always love them.

I believe that if someone has an inclination to seek his birth parents, he should proceed as soon as possible. The sense of closure I experienced was immense and immediate—even before I met my new siblings. My only regret stems from not pursuing the search earlier and harder.

Each day I feel less like an outsider in my new family. I can't imagine my world without them. We e-mail and call one another; we've been lucky to gather for several holidays and events. I've met cousins, aunts, and uncles.

Wayne is warm, thoughtful, and open about calling me "son." I see him as another dad, much as I looked on Shelley's father before he died.

I call three women "Mom." Using the title for the woman who raised me, the one who gave birth to me, and Shelley's mother, seems natural. Since finding my birth mother, my life is full and satisfying, beyond all my expectations. I feel complete knowing the decisions she made were best for us both. I can only look forward—to laughing through more good times together and watching our love grow. And always, to another phone call.

Epilogue

June 2006

You'd think in this age of computers that the Internet would have led Joel's cousin Sarah to find me for him. Just as the timing for my appearance was God's, so was the human way it came about.

Sarah told Joel she would take up the search and use her computer to find me. She was checking a program that lists graduates from various high schools when a driver made a delivery to her home. She knew this man, and as they visited, he asked her where she thought I'd grown up.

"She graduated from Lake George High School, but I can't find any trace of her there."

The driver chuckled, saying he and another driver vacationed at Lake George. In fact, they were taking their families there in a week. "We'll ask around and see if anyone knows the name."

They asked around Lake George Village but couldn't find anyone who remembered a Donna Granger. While they ate lunch and discussed their failure, a woman at the next table approached.

"Excuse, me, I don't mean to eavesdrop, but I was the librarian at the high school. I don't remember her, but I think I know her father. Why don't you take a phone book and call some of the Grangers?"

They took the book home to Sarah. The first home Sarah reached was my brother Dale's.

"Hello. My name is Sarah Herlihy, and I'm trying to locate a Donna Granger."

My niece told Sarah that she had an aunt Donna. "She lives in Texas."

For years, I recited prayers, sang hymns, and listened to the teachings of Jesus at church. In the midst of all this emotional turmoil, I learned a magnificent truth: God's forgiveness is there for the asking. His perfect love bonds us together, forever. Deep within in us, God creates a love for a parent, whether a natural or adoptive one, and it is a strong and beautiful force.

•   •   •

I'd almost finished unloading my cart, when the Walmart cashier glanced up and mumbles a perfunctory, "How are you?" Her ID badge said "Tanisha." Without waiting for my response, she worked in silence, scanning and flipping items into yawning white bags on the carousel.

It was okay this woman in the royal blue smock didn't seem to notice I'd grouped like-items to feed her hungry conveyor. Perhaps Walmart trainers no longer emphasize bread coming from the bottom of a bag shouldn't look like a shoe. Or that apple dents will turn into brown rotten spots, and cracked eggs will super-glue themselves to cartons. Perhaps Tanisha was just tired from the monotonous standing, dealing with faceless customers, and the unending stream rumbling toward her.

I knew how to bring a smile to her impassive face. An unconventional method perhaps, but it came hand-delivered from my heart and seldom failed. As I pushed the emptied cart ahead, I answered her generic greeting. "I'm fantastic, Tanisha, and getting better because every day is Christmas!"

My Walmart audience of one paused, as if processing what this newest fool had just uttered. She didn't respond, but her mask of self-absorption didn't quite slide back into place either.

I intruded before she could disappear again. "Tanisha, don't you want to know *why* every day is Christmas?"

Her large brown eyes locked into mine. Her brows knit together for an instant.

I held her gaze and watched her distrust of a stranger melt away like spring snows.

A slight smile tugged at the corner of her upper lip. "Why?"

In the noisy, too-warm, throbbing universe of super-retail, I began a story that would bring a smile to Tanisha. "So every day is Christmas to me because on June 17, 2004, I received a phone call…"

Mindful of her work, I began sharing the fairy-tale-come-true of a determined little boy who searched for his mother in malls. I relished the wonder spreading across the face before me.

As often happens, the woman queued behind me leaned forward to listen as she slapped items on the black rubber belt. I welcomed her with a smile, noted the goose bumps she was pointing to on her arm, and continued my story.

• • •

I've told our story hundreds of times—to strangers, friends, and church groups. In response, many listeners share their own stories of babies given for adoption, being an adopted child, or an adoptive parent. The story inspires some to seek a parent, some a child.

I now know many women who had more difficulty than I did. On the surface, it might seem otherwise, but none who have shared their experiences made their decisions lightly—even a woman who saw no alternatives but to give up three daughters.

Telling others of Joel's finding me never fails to elicit smiles from the listener and often brings hope and joy, which is why I share the story. But not all stories turn out as ours did. I can't explain why. I only know it's part of God's unfailing grace, and in Him there is always hope. I know he answers prayers, and sometimes it takes hard times to bring us to our knees.

I did what I felt mattered most—I chose not to have my baby aborted, illegally or otherwise.

I chose to allow another mother to love him.

I chose not to look for my son, even as I wept and lamented our separation all those years.

If I could sit across from a pregnant woman who feels ashamed, unprepared, or unwilling for motherhood, I couldn't judge her. I *know* her pain. I would encourage her to embrace hope—for herself, for her child, and for someone else praying for a baby to love. Adoption offers a wondrous answer to unexpected and unplanned circumstances in life. It also offers a path toward healing.

I don't know the Bible as I should. I'm not faithful in my devotions. I sometimes make conscious decisions to not act loving toward others. Yet I know not all of the things that happened to me, and because of me, were of my doing. They were God's time and plan for me, for Joel, for us all.

While we visited Joel in Washington, he took us for a drive one rainy afternoon into the Cascade Mountains. He drove slowly so we could take in the breath-taking, almost primordial scenery. Knowing of Wayne's passion for eagles, he veered onto the shoulder, parked the car, and motioned for us to get out quietly.

The ultimate reminder that God renews our strength through faith sat before us, high in the bare trees. Despite the cold and mist, we stood by the car in awe for half an hour as several magnificent eagles surveyed the rushing stream below for salmon.

Isaiah 40:31 became the verse for the day: "But they that wait upon the Lord shall renew their strength; they shall mount up with wings as eagles…"

The prayer of Jabez *has* expanded my territory. I looked up at Joel's handsome face beside me. *Through all the years I waited for God's answer, all the nights I prayed or cried or wondered about my baby, I listened but never heard Him answer. Still, I refused to give up hope. Thirty-eight years later, I finally heard the song in that silence. I am blessed, indeed.*

Nursing school graduation night, five and a
half months pregnant and terrified

One happy mom with (left to right) Jonathan, Stephanie, and Joel

Our first meeting, July 4, 2004. Front row left to right, Joel's wife Shelley and daughter Mandy, Stephanie and Jonathan. Back row, Joel, Donna, and Wayne.

Shelley, Mandy, and Joel.

Stephanie, Kodi, and Kevin

Joel, Donna, Stephanie, and Jonathan, Thanksgiving 2005

Donna G. Paul

Joel meets Congressman Ron Paul who presents flag flown over the Capitol on Joel's birthday. As Shelley looks on, Joel says, "Momma, you keep making me cry."

You've Got To Read This! (YGTRT!)
Selling books is a hundred times more challenging than writing one. If I find a writer who has a way with words, like Andy Andrews in *The Butterfly Effect,* I spread the news. If I post an author's name on my Facebook, blog, or Twitter followed by YGTRT I hope you read it.

If you enjoyed *A Song in Every Silence*, pass it along with your own YGTRTs. Maybe you and I can start something here. I'd love to hear from you via donna@donnagpaul.com.
Thank you for reading, Donna